Planning Jerusalem

Planning Jerusalem

The Master Plan for the Old City of Jerusalem and Its Environs

By Arieh Sharon

Planning Team of the Outline Townplanning Scheme:
Arieh Sharon, David Anatol Brutzkus, Eldar Sharon
Architects and Townplanners

Art Editor and Design: Chava Mordohovich

McGraw-Hill Book Company

New York	Kuala Lumpur	Panama
St. Louis	London	Rio de Janeiro
San Francisco	Mexico	Singapore
Düsseldorf	Montreal	Sydney
Johannesburg	New Delhi	Toronto

Sponsors: The Ministry of the Interior of the State of Israel
and the Municipality of Jerusalem
Professional Committee: Ya'akov Dash, B. Arch., A.M.T.P.I.,
Head of Planning Department Ministry of the Interior;
Ammikam Yafeh, City Engineer Municipality of Jerusalem

**Library of Congress
Cataloging in Publication Data**

Sharon, Arieh,
Planning Jerusalem.
"Sponsors: the Ministry of the Interior and the
Municipality of Jerusalem."
Bibliography: p.
1. Cities and towns—Planning—Jerusalem.
I. Brutzkus, David Anatol. II. Sharon, Eldar.
III. Israel. Misrad ha-penim. IV. Jerusalem,
Israel. V. Title.
NA9265.S48   309.2'62'0956944   73—8521

Published in Israel by
Weidenfeld and Nicolson Jerusalem
19 Herzog Street   Jerusalem
Published in Great Britain by
Weidenfeld and Nicolson
11 St. John's Hill   London SW 11

Composed and bound by Keter Press, Jerusalem
Map Separation and Plates by Reshet-Kav, Givatayim
Printed by Japhet Press, Tel Aviv, Israel
ISF

Contents

Foreword
Chapter 1   The Townplanning Area 3
Chapter 2   The Plan in the Context of History 13
Chapter 3   The Landscape 31
Chapter 4   The Walls and Gates of Jerusalem 45
Chapter 5   Structure and Architecture of the Old City 79
Chapter 6   The Old City Survey and Outline Scheme 109
Chapter 7   Earlier Townplanning Schemes 125
Chapter 8   The Outline Scheme of the Special Zone 137
Chapter 9   Projects 161

Introduction

Eternity — that is Jerusalem. This Saying of the Sages reflects something of the unique and sanctified place which Jerusalem has always occupied in the hearts of every member of the House of Israel. To them it is the eternal city, capital of Israel ever since the first kingdom of Israel was established there three thousand years ago. Its uniqueness and sanctity have been given an added dimension with its re-unification after the Six Day War in 1967.

Centre of the reborn State of Israel, of Judaism and of Jewish nationhood, Jerusalem is also a city sacred to Christianity and Islam. Its religious, archaeological and historical sites are held in reverence by peoples of all three faiths throughout the world. Their spirits are quickened by the very utterance of its name.

The Ministry of the Interior and the Municipality of Jerusalem have together embarked on a masterplan for the Old City designed to preserve its unique values, status and treasure, past and present. While taking account of modern urban needs, this plan seeks meticulously to safeguard the spirit, the character and the sites of antiquity of this remarkable city.

It is my hope that this masterplan will bring honour to the State of Israel and to the House of Israel, evocative of the biblical 'Jerusalem, built as a city which is bound together firmly' (Psalms 122:3).

Dr Josef Burg
Minister of Interior

The Old City of Jerusalem is unique. Its religious, historical, archaeological and architectural treasures are part of the world's heritage. At the same time it is the home of thousands of people, of adherents of the three great religions, of Jews, Moslems and Christians, of young and old. The Municipality of Jerusalem, together with the Ministry of the Interior, present herein a proposal for the future of this area, which holds so much significance for so many.

As this is being written, the Outline Townplanning Scheme for the Old City of Jerusalem and its environs is in the process of being presented to the appropriate legal authorities on its journey to becoming law. We believe it is only proper to offer the plan simultaneously to the wider public, to the people of the world who hold the Old City in reverence, so that they too may be a part of the Jerusalem of the future.

The Outline Townplanning Scheme is based upon a similar reverence on the part of the planners. Its fundamental purpose is to grant honour and recognition to the past, to the centuries and peoples who have created the Old City and who have endowed it with its present form and style.

Yet the Old City of Jerusalem is not only the site of Holy Places. It is also the place where history and the exigencies of modern life meet. For the first time, the past century has seen the building of a metropolis outside the walls of the ancient city. Today, the old and the new are two parts of a whole. They face the same problems — a population explosion, the need for more housing, for more and better schools and for the amenities of urban life. Equally important, all of the city requires a better quality of life for its inhabitants. This quality can be enhanced by preserving the beauty that is Jerusalem, its valleys and landscapes, its vistas and parks.

The Outline Townplanning Scheme provides for a city which will be able to service its inhabitants. It provides for an ambiance reflecting the juxtaposition of the old and the new. It preserves without stultify-ing; allows for innovation without risking offence.

The preservation of the walls of the Old City was an ideal of those who tried to direct the future of Jerusalem a half century ago and were the first who consciously tried to maintain the character of the city. The current proposal protects the advances towards this goal which have been made recently and carries them forward so that the walls will stand majestically unhindered and uncluttered.

Moreover, the National Park surrounding the Old City — first envisaged in the original plan for the city over fifty years ago — is an integral part of the current plan. The need for such an open space to prevent encroachment is more necessary today than ever before, and its beginnings must be continued.

Thus, the plan that is presented in the following pages envisages a living city, a unity between the old and the new. We hope that those who study it will understand how important the Old City is to us who must plan for it; how much we have sacrificed and are willing to continue to sacrifice for its sake. We hope that we can continue to advance and progress along the long road that lies ahead of us and that we will have the aid of men of goodwill everywhere in our task.

Teddy Kollek
Mayor of Jerusalem

מבוא

והנצח – זו ירושלים. יש באמרה זו משום ביטוי לערכי היחוד והקדושה אשר עם ישראל רוחש לעיר הנצח ירושלים, בירת ישראל מיום שנתכוננה בה מלכות ישראל לראשונה.

לייחודה של ירושלים יש משנה תוקף עם איחודה מחדש לעיר אחת לאחר מלחמת ששת הימים בשנת 1967. יחד עם היותה לבירתה של מדינת ישראל המחודשת, הרי היא משמשת כעיר קדושה ליהדות, לנצרות ולאיסלאם. אתריה הדתיים, הארכיאולוגיים וההיסטוריים משמשים מקור להשראה רוחנית לכל עמי תבל.

משרד-הפנים ועיריית ירושלים חברו יחדיו להכנת תכנית-מתאר לירושלים העתיקה, אשר תשלב בתוכה שמירה על ערכי הייחוד של ירושלים בעבר ובהווה. יש בתכנית זו משום ביטוי לצרכים של הזמנים החדשים של העיר, אך יחד עם זאת היא מבטאת את השמירה המעולה על אתריה, רוחה ואפיה.

אני מקווה כי תכנית זו תהא לתפארת למדינת ישראל ולעם ישראל, בבחינת "ירושלים הבנויה כעיר שחברה לה יחדו" (תהלים קכ"ב ג').

ד"ר יוסף בורג
שר-הפנים

העיר העתיקה של ירושלים מיוחדת-במינה היא. אוצרות הייחודה, ההיסטוריה, הארכיאולוגיה והארכיטקטורה שלה הינם חלק של המורשה העולמית. בד-בבד הריהי מעונם של אלפי בני-אדם, של מאמיני שלושת הדתות הגדולות, של יהודים, מוסלמים ונוצרים, של צעירים וקשישים.

בעת כתיבתם של דברים אלה מצויה תכנית-המתאר של ירושלים וסביבותיה בתהליך הגשתה לרשויות התכנוניות המתאימות, במטרה להפכה למסמך חוקי. אנו סבורים שאך יאה הוא להציג את התכנית בעת-ובעונה-אחת בפני הציבור הרחב, בפני אוכלוסי העולם הרוחשים רגש עז ויראה לעיר העתיקה, כדי שיוכלו גם הם להיות חלק של ירושלים הזאת של העתיד.

תכנית-המתאר מבוססת על רחשי-יראה דומים מצד מתכנניה. יסוד-תכליתה הוא מתן כבוד והכרה לעבר, לאותן מאות-שנים ולאותם אנשים אשר יצרו את העיר העתיקה ואשר העניקו לה את צורתה וסיגנונה בהווה.

אולם העיר העתיקה איננה אך ורק אתר של מקומות קדושים. היא גם המקום שבו נפגשת ההיסטוריה עם צווי החיים המודרניים. לראשונה ראתה המאה הקודמת בבנייתה של מטרופולין מחוץ לחומות העיר הקדומה. היום, הישן והחדש הם שני חלקים של יחידה אחת. עומדים הם בפני אותן הבעיות – התפוצצות אוכלוסין, הצורך בבתי-מגורים רבים יותר, בבתי-ספר טובים ורבים יותר ובמימוש היתרונות של החיים בעיר. מידה דומה של חשיבות נודעת להשבחת איכות-החיים של תושבי העיר כולה. איכות זו ניתן להגבירה על-ידי שמירת יופיה של ירושלים – עמקיה ונופיה, מראיה וגניה.

שמירת חומותיה של העיר העתיקה היתה משאת-נפשם של אלה אשר ניסו לכוון את עתידה של ירושלים לפני מחצית-המאה ואשר היו הראשונים שניסו במודע לשמר את אופיה של העיר. ההצעה הנוכחית מקיימת את ההתקרבות שנעשתה לאחרונה לקראת המטרה הזאת ומקדמת אותה באופן שהחומות נישאות תהיינה במלוא פאר-הדרן, בלא כל מכשול ופגע.

יתר על כן, הגן הלאומי המכתר את העיר העתיקה – אשר לראשונה נחזה בתכנית המקורית של העיר חמשים שנה קודם-לכן – הוא חלק מהותי של התכנית הנוכחית.

הצורך במרחב פתוח באזור הזה הוא חיוני היום יותר משהיה אי-פעם בעבר ומן ההכרח שיבוא המשך לראשוני צעדיו.

כך אפוא מעלה מגלה התכנית המוגשת בעמודים הבאים עיר חיה, איחוד הישן עם החדש. אנו תקוה כי אלה אשר יעיינו בה יבינו עד כמה חשובה היא העיר העתיקה לנו החיים בה לתכננה; כמה הרבה הקרבנו וכמה הרבה מוכנים אנו להוסיף ולהקריב למענה. אנו תקוה כי נוכל לצעוד ולהתקדם בדרך הארוכה המצפה לנו, וכי נזכה לעזרה במשימתנו מצד אנשים בעלי רצון טוב באשר הינם.

טדי קולק
ראש עיריית ירושלים

Foreword

Ten measures of beauty descended from the heavens — nine were taken by Jerusalem and one by the rest of the world (The Talmud).

The challenge was exciting — and awesome: to conceive a townplanning design for the Old City of Jerusalem and its environs, a three-dimensional architectural design of this special area which, though relatively small, is so rich and colourful in its landscape and so intensive in its townscape. Nowhere in the world does so compact an area contain so rare and rich a treasury of historic buildings, monuments and associations of such sensitive concern to so many peoples in the world.

Jerusalem is the centre of two great monotheistic religions, Judaism and Christianity, and the third Holy Place of Islam. To members of those faiths, every stone, the smallest patch of ground, is hallowed. For Jews, the Old City was given a unique significance by King David and King Solomon in the tenth century BC and by a dramatic and fateful recorded history of three thousand years; for Christians, it was given an ineluctable reverence by the final ministry of Jesus almost two thousand years ago; and its association with a dream of Mohammed thirteen centuries ago made it a venerated site for Moslems. Whatever is done in Jerusalem and its environs excites the sensitivities of the faithful of these three religions, wherever in the world they may live.

But Jerusalem is also the home of more than a quarter of a million inhabitants. It is a living city. It thrives, today more than ever. It grows. How is this new expansion to be effected without disturbing the special character with which it has been invested by its matchless history and the variegated architecture of past centuries?

Even the small walled-in Old City of Jerusalem is a lively residential and commercial centre with a population of 24,000 on a small area of 215 acres. Unlike many walled-in medieval cities of Europe which still exist, the Old City is a vivid and lively urban organism,

full of people of various races and religions who live, study, work and spend their leisure hours within its walls.

There is also a special beauty about the Old City of Jerusalem, the wondrous beauty of a city set amidst the timeless terraces and hills of Judea, perched on hillocks, surrounded by magnificent stone ramparts, skirted by ravines and faced by the gentle slopes of the Mount of Olives and Mount Scopus with their commanding view of the plain of Jericho, the Jordan River and the Dead Sea. How does one preserve this beauty, yet provide modern amenities for a growing population and for the hundreds of thousands of annual visitors who are drawn to this centre of pilgrimage in increasing numbers?

To conserve the old and bring forth the full measure of its magnificence; to conceive the new with a sense of history so that it blends with its ancient surroundings; and to enhance and add a dimension to the special character of this city of antiquity and scenic beauty — these were the challenges presented to the Jerusalem townplanners.

Shortly after the Six Day War in 1967, when Jerusalem became a reunited city, the task of preparing an architectural townplanning scheme for the Old City and its environs was entrusted to our planning team. From the very start, after touring and studying the Old City and its surroundings, and particularly after our surveys and research into the physical and historical factors and the socio-economic conditions, it became clear that our planning activities had to encompass three primary goals: to preserve the townscape and character of the walled city proper; to protect the superb landscape of the deep valleys of Hinnom and Kidron adjacent to the city walls, with the gentle slopes of Mount Scopus and the Mount of Olives in the background; and to establish an organic architectural and functional relation between the Old City and the new quarters of Jerusalem immediate to its north and north-west.

The Old City forms an irregular square of about 900 by 900 metres surrounded by strong and impressive walls, rebuilt at the beginning of the sixteenth century by Suleiman the Magnificent. Its population today is about 24,000, but it is visited daily by many thousands of Jerusalemites and tourists — in some weeks the number of visitors exceeds 100,000.

Throughout the centuries, the Old City has been largely a pedestrian city. The interior distance between the walls, averaging 750 metres to 900 metres, allows both inhabitants and visitors to reach their destination on foot: the children and students their schools, the residents their shops and workshops, the visitors their churches, mosques or synagogues and the bazaars. As of old, donkeys, mules and small carts have remained the conventional means of transport — most of the narrow streets and alleys are in any case too steep (and many of them have steps) for the passage of vehicles. Only in a few places is motor traffic possible: near the New Gate, Jaffa Gate and the Dung Gate, where a breach was made in the existing wall through which cars may enter, although their movement through the winding alleys and narrow lanes is a hindrance to pedestrians. One of our aims was to restore to the city its former character and charm, to preserve the residential and commercial streets (many of them still neat and clean) with their stone-built façades, their quiet interior courtyards, their public buildings and small piazzas and to rid them of their modernistic additions, such as canopies and shutters, which were added mostly in the commercial streets and bazaars of the Moslem and Christian quarters. It was also our aim to rebuild the completely destroyed houses and synagogues of the Jewish Quarter; to clear the slums in the Moslem Quarter and provide new housing schemes for its crowded population; to provide parking places and garages near the main city gates and to prohibit traffic within the Old City during daytime (only in the early morning and late evening is service and emergency traffic to be allowed).

The landscape round the Old City is particularly variegated, impressive and attractive. The magnificent city walls, which consist partly of natural rock foundations, partly of huge stone blocks (remnants of the Herodian wall) and for the most part of regular stonework of the sixteenth century are skirted in the east, south and west by the steep ravines and valleys of Hinnom and Kidron. These valleys have preserved their natural character of stony slopes, with coppices, vineyards, olive groves, ancient buildings and the picturesque village of Siloam in the south and the charming Yemin Moshe Quarter in the west almost intact. Fortunately, a government decision came to the planners' aid, designating these valleys and the adjacent slopes a National Park area comprising 500 acres. Under the care of the National Parks Authority, this area is to be developed as a public park and garden. Historical monuments are to be preserved and new pedestrian paths and gardens are to be planted in harmony with the existing landscape and topography. The Siloam village and the Yemin Moshe Quarter are to be restored.

The background to the Kidron Valley, Mount Scopus, the Mount of Olives, the Mount of Offence and Government House Hill is partly built-up with residential quarters and public and religious buildings. These hilly ridges are to be developed into organic neighbourhood units in such a way as to achieve a harmonious skyline along the crest. Mount Scopus will house the enlarged campus of the Hebrew University.

The most difficult and delicate architectural problem is to create an organic correlation between the Old City and new Jerusalem along the northern wall and the northern part of the western wall, where the residential and commercial quarters of new Jerusalem almost touch the city walls, being separated only by a narrow and crowded motor-road. Located here are the main gates, Jaffa Gate and Damascus Gate, the points of entry into the Old City of the main roads from the west and the north. Fortunately, free and open areas between these two city gates and the densely built-up urban areas nearby still exist. These

areas can contribute to the solution of one of the vital architectural problems — that of connecting the old with the new — for they are natural meeting points. They will provide underground parking for thousands of cars (which will not be allowed to enter the Old City) and also offer intermediate services — civic and commercial centres — for residents and visitors.

It was not part of our purpose to convert the Old City and its immediate environs into a frozen historical monument, nor to turn it into a museum piece, rather to preserve it as it is — a lively urban organism — while restoring its former character as a city of pedestrians moving freely and unimpeded from house to house, shop to shop, from home to school, to mosque, church or synagogue, and from the gates and piazzas to the bazaars, as was the pattern in earlier generations. Streets and piazzas, the lifelines and living cores of urban civilization, have degenerated in the last few decades into a labyrinth of motor lanes and highways. The once popular art of walking, of enjoying the indoor-outdoor atmosphere of sidewalk cafés and shops, of gardens and vaulted alleyways, of fountains, courts and paved piazzas, of absorbing the lively, colourful scenes in the decorative streets, the very charm of a Mediterranean city — all seem to have been forgotten, as has the spontaneous joy of people communicating freely with each other. Here we were faced with the challenge to re-introduce spiritual and physical values to a small but vibrant pedestrian town and re-endow it with its historical enchantment: to integrate it into the gracious landscape of deep valleys and gentle hills round the city walls; and to link it organically with the built-up areas in the north and north-west to form an integral architectural entity.

A. Sh.

1

Chapter 1   The Townplanning Area

The Townplanning Area

With the reunification of Jerusalem in 1967, the Ministry of the Interior and the Municipality of Jerusalem decided to prepare a townplanning scheme for the Old City of Jerusalem and its immediate environs. The task of devising this townplanning scheme was entrusted to the architects Arieh Sharon, David Anatol Brutzkus and Eldar Sharon, who set up a special design and planning team for this purpose. This team worked in close contact with Mr Ya'akov Dash, head of the Townplanning Department in the Ministry of the Interior, Mr Ammikam Yafeh, the City Engineer of Jerusalem, and other municipal and government planning agencies. At the same time, the Government and Municipality appointed a special Townplanning Commission with the primary function of approving building and other development activities within this planning area.

The area concerned covers some 10.5 square kilometres and constitutes only a comparatively small part — roughly 10% — of the municipal area of Greater Jerusalem. Its boundaries are: on the west, the densely built-up areas of the new Jewish city; on the east, the steep and arid slopes of the Judean Hills overlooking the Dead Sea; on the north, the residential and commercial Arab quarters; on the south, the residential and business quarters of the new city.

Lying within these bounds of the townplanning scheme, indeed its very heart, is the Old City of Jerusalem, whose walls enclose an irregular square about 900 by 900 metres, with an area of 215 acres (one acre equals four dunams). These formidable walls — rising on foundations of natural rock with the huge stone blocks of the Herodian period among some of its courses, but consisting for the most part of massive masonry built to a height of 8 to 12 metres five hundred years ago — are the principal reason for the preservation to this very day of the medieval character of the Old City. Another reason is the absence of motor traffic within the walls — with the exception of some roads in the Christian and Armenian quarters which are disturbing to the unique personality of the Old City. This apart, the Old City's streets, alleys, courtyards and piazzas have preserved their traditional character. The buildings are all in local stone, one to two storeys high, merging into a homogeneous visual space of quiet, winding, residential streets and lively, noisy bazaars, and are interspersed with higher public and religious buildings with their spires, towers and domes matching the townscape. Only the slums of the Moslem Quarter need urgent renewal and clearance. The destroyed Jewish Quarter calls for immediate reconstruction.

It is the Old City and its immediate surroundings, notably the Valley of Hinnom on its west and south and on its east the Valley of Kidron and the slopes of the Mount of Olives, Mount Scopus, the Mount of Offence and Government House Hill, which have received prime attention in the townplanning scheme. These valleys are partly covered with pine trees and vegetable plots, while some of the terraced slopes are planted with vines, olive and cypress trees, though most of them are barren, eroded and rocky and are covered with ancient cemeteries close to the city wall. These valleys and hills form the visual architectural space of the area, with their dramatic views of the Old City — and vice versa. The entire scenery changes hourly throughout the year — with the specific intensive and colourful light and bright sunshine on Jerusalem's hills and valleys. The whole area, including the Old City, is rich in ancient sites, in relics of the biblical past and in monuments and places of worship of all three religions which were erected over the centuries, many of them on the foundations of much earlier structures.

A number of townplanning schemes for Jerusalem were prepared during the period of British rule in Palestine between 1918 and 1948. They are presented and considered in chapter VII. Some of their recommendations were put into effect, such as restoring certain historic buildings within the Old City, preserving the city walls, restricting the height of buildings and ensuring that only local stone be used for construction. But this was a period of tension, often erupting into wide-spread hostilities between Arabs and Jews and between both communities and the British Administration, and no major progress could be made on the plans as a whole, covering the broad environs of the city.

In 1948 came the Arab attack on the newly established State of Israel, and Israel had to fight its War of Independence. The end of the war was marked by Armistice Agreements early in 1949, and the armistice lines with the Kingdom of Jordan (then Transjordan) bisected Jerusalem into east and west, with the Old City falling under Jordanian control. Each country developed its part of Jerusalem in its own way, but while Israel produced its masterplan in 1950 guiding the city's planning and development and the Jerusalem Outline Scheme in 1959, the Arab part was allowed to grow in haphazard fashion throughout the nineteen years of Jordanian rule. During that time, many buildings were erected without regard to height and surroundings on the slopes of the Mount of Olives and in Siloam village.

Only with the reunification of the city after the Six Day War were conditions ripe for the preparation of a comprehensive townplanning scheme — and its implementation by a determined Government of Israel and Municipality of Jerusalem — covering the entire area of the Old City and its environs and treating it as an organic, unified whole.

The proposed townplanning scheme had to consider the usual aspects of a regulative scheme: use of land, communications network, public and private open spaces and areas for residential, religious and public buildings, schools, sport and recreation. The planners accordingly prepared detailed surveys of topographical, geographical, historical, demographic and socio-economic data for each of the twenty units into which the planning area was subdivided (see page 140). The boundaries of these planning units were mostly determined by topographical, demographic and architectural factors. In each of the units, the future size of population was indicated, based on development possibilities in accordance with the proposed scheme.

The planners sought to co-ordinate their regulative proposals concerning land usage, communications and the nature, density and height of building with the three-dimensional space aspects of the whole area. It was therefore proposed to devise detailed schemes and architectural projects which would be governed by the space relations between existing and projected built-up areas and the surrounding landscape of hills and valleys, so as to suit the building silhouette to the hilly skyline and achieve a harmonious and organic landscape and townscape.

In preparing this plan, the designers had to take account of historical and archaeological features which are often the crucial ingredients in the character of a region, and particularly so in this area, which bears the indelible impact of the various periods of its history. Considerable future archaeological excavation is planned, and the development scheme makes provision for this. The numerous recent excavations have brought to light relics of the past, bringing to vivid life the words in the Bible and the writings of later periods.

Panoramic aerial photograph of the Old City of Jerusalem and its environs

Municipal Boundary

Planning Area

Old City

Planning Area Boundary

Old City

Valleys

Ridges

1 Boundary of Municipal Area
2 Boundary of Special Zone
3 The Van Leer Three-Dimensional
   Map of the Old City

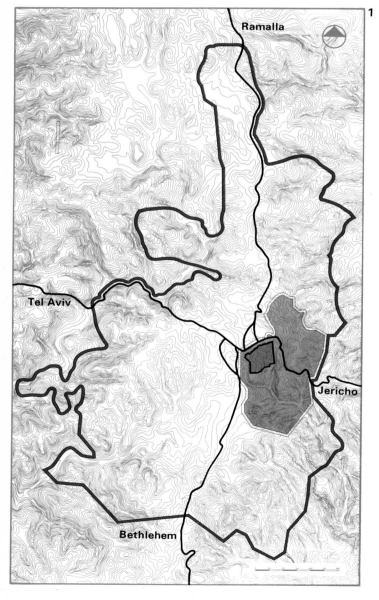

Ramalla

Tel Aviv

Jericho

Bethlehem

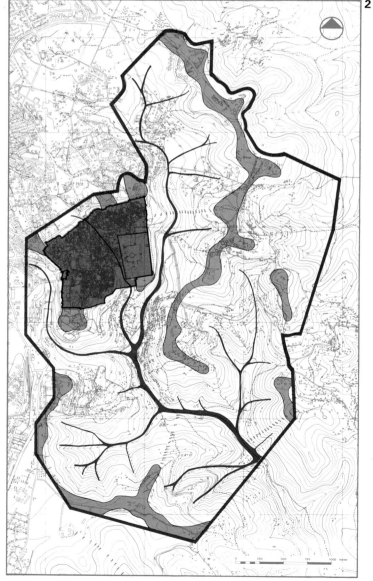

The Geographic Setting of Jerusalem

1   Photograph of Middle East, taken by
    astronauts Michael Collins and John
    Young on Gemini 10 flight in July 1966
2   Map of Palestine, Antwerp, 1579
3   A 16th-century map of Palestine,
    emphasizing the position of Jerusalem on
    the watershed between the Dead Sea and
    the Mediterranean
4   Map of Judea and of the Dead Sea,
    London, 1650
5   Franz von Hoghenberg's Map of
    Jerusalem, c. 1580

In the Middle East

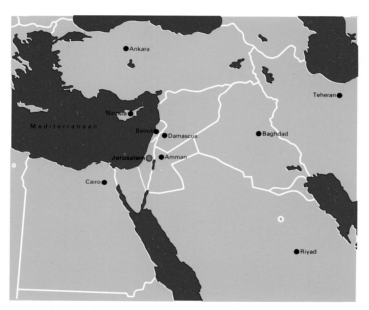

In Israel

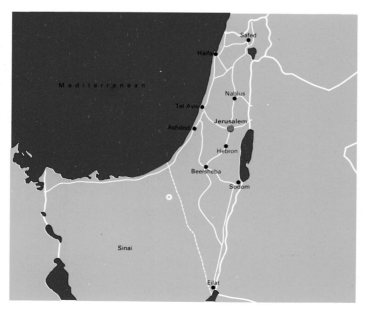

In the Region

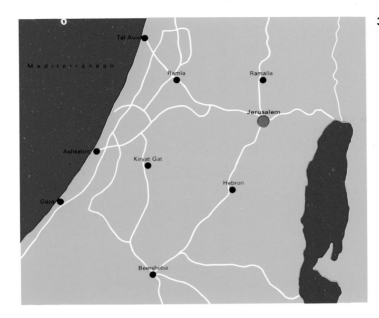

In the Metropolitan Area

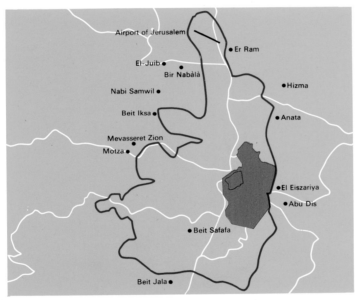

The Special Zone

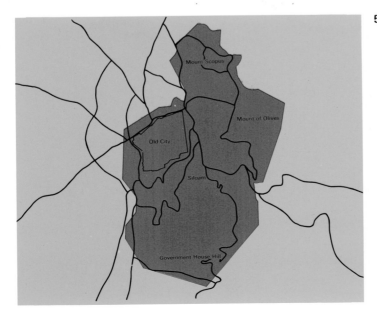

Chapter 2   The Plan in the Context of History

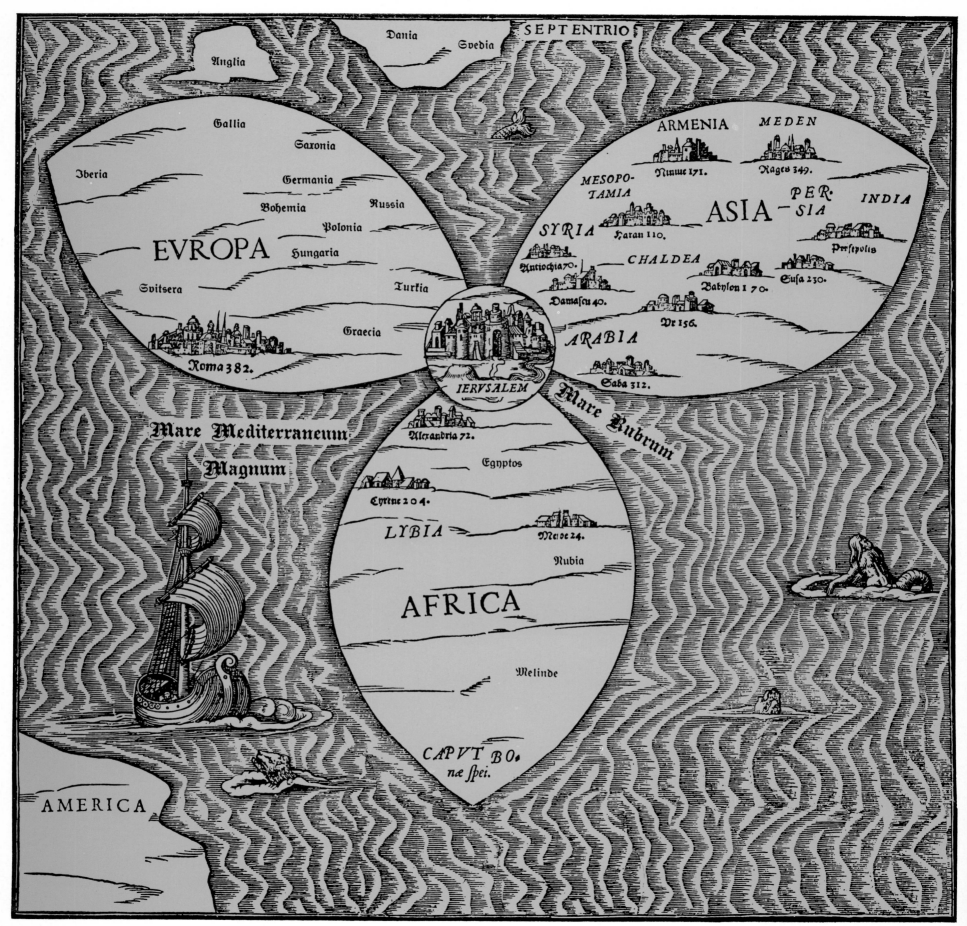

SEPTENTRIO

Dania   Svedia

Anglia

Gallia   ARMENIA   MEDEN
                Saxonia
Iberia   Niniue 171.   Rages 349.
                Germania   MESOPO-
        Bohemia   Russia   TAMIA   ASIA   PER-   INDIA
                Polonia   SYRIA   SIA
EVROPA   Hungaria   Haran 110.   CHALDEA   Perspolis
                Antiochia 70.   Susa 230.
Svitsera   Damascu 40.   Babylon 170.
                Turkia   Vr 156.
        Graecia   ARABIA
    Roma 382.   IERVSALEM   Saba 312.

Mare Mediterraneum   Mare Rubrum
                    Alexandria 72.
Magnum
                Egyptos

        Cyrene 204.
                LYBIA   Meroe 24.
                        Nubia

            AFRICA

                Melinde

        CAPVT BO-
            næ spei.

AMERICA

14

The Plan in the Context of History

One of the primary aims of the townplanning scheme is to enable the Jerusalem resident and visitor to move through the Old City and its environs with a tangible sense of the dramatic historic events and development of this unique city. It was thus essential to set the plan in the authentic context of Jerusalem's history. The planners were aided in achieving this goal by three illuminating instruments: the written records; the existing structures; and the archaeological discoveries.

The written records, like Jerusalem itself, are unique in several respects. There is an abundant, almost uninterrupted, documentation on the history of Jerusalem over the last three thousand years (and even some written material on the earlier centuries). The principal source, covering for the most part much of the first millennium BC, is the Bible. The books of the Talmud cover the immediate post-biblical centuries. The works of the first century AD historian Josephus Flavius give extraordinary details of the buildings and the eventful years in the city during his lifetime; they also contain much that is valuable on the Herodian period. The changing patterns in the look and life of the city, with special attention paid to the architectural development in each major period, were amply set down throughout the subsequent nineteen centuries in the journals of articulate pilgrims and the writings of other travellers. Many ancient structures that still stand bear witness to these historical reports, and recent archaeological discoveries have both confirmed many of the ancient texts and shed light on obscurities which had long baffled historians.

Jerusalem and its history are unique in other respects. Jerusalem is the only city of consequence in the world which enjoys none of the physical features that were the normal attributes of a great town in ages past — strategic location, abundance of water, proximity to caravan routes and rich natural resources. Jerusalem commands no great river or important highway and overlooks no great harbour. It was never the key to the conquest of prized territory. It had certain blessed qualities not given to all — beauty, an equable climate, a modest water supply, pure air and a luminous quality to its light which must have awed the ancients as it does the modern visitor. But these were not sufficient to have made it anything more than a feasible and attractive site of early settlement. Jerusalem was made great by the statesmen, prophets, poets and philosophers of ancient days.

Its first mention in the written records appears in the nineteenth-century BC Egyptian Execration Texts, when, as usual throughout the second millennium BC, Jerusalem was in thrall to one of the two contending empires, the northern or the southern, of the early Near East. The Bible records the Patriarch Abraham's association with Jerusalem in the eighteenth century BC, when it was a city of Canaanites (Genesis 14:8). Among the fourteenth-century BC Tel el-Amarna letters are some from the ruler of Jerusalem. Only with the successful assault by King David at the beginning of the tenth century BC, however, did it become an Israelite city. Its history of importance dates from that epoch.

The City of David and Solomon and the First Temple Period, 1000 — 587 BC

opposite *Jerusalem and the Temple, centre, as depicted in a wood-cut published in Nürnberg in 1493*

It was David who developed Jerusalem, built up its fortifications, erected impressive public buildings and made it the political capital of the kingdom of Israel, which, under his rule, extended from the Red Sea in the south to the Euphrates in the north and beyond Transjordan in the east. But perhaps of more lasting significance was his bringing of the Ark of the Covenant to Jerusalem and providing a permanent resting place for this most sacred national and religious symbol of Israel on the highest spot in the hill-city, the traditional Mount Moriah. (At the time, this was the 'threshing floor of Araunah the Jebusite' [II Samuel 24:18], and though it had been offered to him as a gift, David insisted on buying it.) Jerusalem thus became not only the political but also the religious capital, and it was to remain for all time the spiritual centre of the nation.

The Jerusalem of David's day was located south of today's Old City on a hill known as Ophel Hill. (Recent archaeological excavations show that its northern wall was some 650 feet south of today's southern wall.) Its southern wall was at the Pool of Siloam. It was a long and narrow city, its defences based on steep natural inclines in the east (the Kidron Valley), the west (the Central Valley, later known as the Tyropoeon Valley) and the south (the Valley of Hinnom) and on a fortified rampart in the north. The main source of water was the Gihon Spring, in the Kidron Valley. The biblical 'spring' of En-Rogel, further south, was one of several subsidiary sources. Rainwater was stored in pits and cisterns.

Of the structures built in Jerusalem by David, the Bible mentions the royal palace, constructed of stone and cedar; barracks for his garrison troops; accommodation for the members of the royal family, the priests and the royal officials; and a royal tomb for himself and his dynasty.

The City of David was extended considerably northwards by Solomon, and he added magnificence to the structural work started by his father. Enclosed within this enlarged city was the site David had acquired from Araunah, and upon this site Solomon erected his most important and most imposing building — the Temple, a thick-walled, rectangular structure of squared stones and cedar beams, lying from east to west, about 110 feet long, 48 feet broad and more than 50 feet high. A large porch extended on its eastern side and 'side chambers' were built against the other three sides. A partition wall inside the Temple marked off the main hall from 'the oracle . . . to set there the ark of the covenant of the Lord' (I Kings 6:19). From the biblical account, the Temple was certainly the most impressive building in the land, fashioned from the finest materials obtainable in the region, and the architectural details reflected the exquisite workmanship of master craftsmen. But its heart, the 'oracle' containing the Ark, was a gloomy, sombre cubicle, believed to be 'inhabited' by, but containing no image of, the Supreme Being, and at the dedication ceremony, after the Ark had been reverently laid in the darkness of this inner chamber and 'the cloud filled the house of the Lord', the people of Israel standing in the court outside worshipped His presence while Solomon pronounced the nature of the One God (I Kings 8). Through his words and those of the later prophets, the Temple and the city of Jerusalem were to be invested with a unique sacredness, fount of the Jewish religion and central inspiration of the Jewish nation, long after the Temple had been destroyed, and throughout all the centuries of the Jewish exile.

What is today known as the Dome of the Rock (Haram esh-Sharif to the Moslems) is indeed the very site on which Solomon built the Temple, and it is today, as it was in his day, the most spectacular site in Jerusalem. Annexed to the Temple, and separated from it by a wall, rose another formidable building, Solomon's palace. The entire complex was encircled by a strong stone wall, giving it the appearance of a separate citadel within the ramparts of Jerusalem.

Solomon did much to advance the material prosperity of the country and his efforts were reflected in the physical enrichment of the capital. Economic and cultural progress, together with increased contact — through trade and diplomatic alliances — with the best of what other societies had to offer, led to new building techniques, new materials, new construction methods and improved water systems.

With the death of Solomon, political disunity struck the country and the united kingdom founded by David and made prosperous by Solomon was now divided into the kingdom of Israel in the north and the kingdom of Judah in the south. Jerusalem remained the capital of Judah alone. Its political and economic fortunes declined, but its spiritual strength was to be massively fortified by the words and deeds of the Hebrew prophets, particularly by the two giants who lived and uttered their sublime thoughts in Jerusalem, Isaiah and Jeremiah.

Scholars have long known that in the next few centuries the Jerusalem of David and Solomon developed westwards from the Temple Mount. But not until now was it discovered how far west and at how early a date. Shortly after the Six Day War, Prof. Binyamin Mazar of the Hebrew University began extensive archaeological excavations at the southwestern corner of the Temple Compound, and Prof. Nahman Avigad of the Hebrew University began excavating in the Jewish Quarter of the Old City. Mazar found potsherds belonging to the seventh century BC, and one of them, the handle of a jar, bore the Hebrew inscription 'la-melech' — 'For [or of] the King'. He also found two superbly preserved rock-cut chambers to the west of the Western Wall. Avigad's finds, much further to the west, included the seventh-century BC plastered floor, with pottery belonging to the period, of one of the first Israelite houses built in the area. A little while later he discovered part of the seventh-century BC foundations of a city wall, and this was presumably the western boundary of Jerusalem in a century which began with the reign of the redoubtable Hezekiah and ended shortly after the reign of Josiah 'the righteous'. These archaeological discoveries prove conclusively that Jewish settlement began as early as the seventh century BC to extend

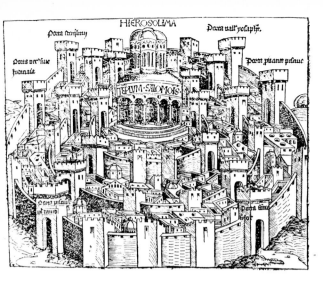

westward from the Temple Mount and Ophel Hill to a ridge parallel to that of the Temple Compound and separated from it by the Central (the Tyropoeon) Valley. (This valley filled up and was built upon during the course of subsequent centuries, so that today there is hardly any break between this former western extension and the earlier biblical city.)

Solomon's Temple and the city of Jerusalem were destroyed by the Babylonian emperor Nebuchadnezzar in 586 BC. Seeking also to destroy any prospect of Jerusalem's ever again becoming the centre of Jewish life, Nebuchadnezzar carried off many of the surviving Jews to Babylon. But there, 'by the waters of Babylon', the exiled Jews vowed, in a cry which has echoed down all the centuries of Jewish history: 'If I forget thee, O Jerusalem, let my right hand forget her cunning . . .' (Psalm 137). About fifty years later, when the Babylonian Empire was conquered by Cyrus, founder of a new Persian Empire, they returned to Jerusalem, with the blessings of Cyrus, to rebuild their Temple.

1   The Temple and the Royal Palace
2   Tombs
3   The Valley Gate
4   The Gihon Spring
5   Hezekiah's Tunnel
6   Siloam Tunnel
7   Royal Tombs
8   Siloam Pool
9   Newly Discovered Wall
    Sites where First Temple
    deposits were found

Jerusalem during the Second Temple Period, 537 BC – AD 70

opposite *A late 16th-century pictorial map of Jerusalem made in Cologne with a view of the city and Second Temple to the right*

Placed in charge of this 'Return to Zion' movement in 537 BC was 'Sheshbazzar, the prince of Judah', considered by scholars to have been a son of Jehoiachin, the exiled boy-king of Judah, and thus the legitimate heir to the throne of Judah. Under Sheshbazzar and his nephew Zerubbabel, who followed him as 'Governor of Judah', the returnees started the slow and painful work of rehabilitating life in the devastated city. In their construction work they applied themselves almost exclusively to the rebuilding of the Temple, and it was completed in 515 BC. It was to stand for almost the next six centuries, right up to AD 70, when it was finally destroyed.

At the time of its completion, the Second Temple, built to the same design as the First, though not as ornate, may have seemed more impressive. For it was now the sole great edifice in a city whose walls lay in ruins, and it stood alone upon the high ground, set in its own courts and surrounded by its own wall. As the nineteenth-century historian George Adam Smith pointed out, it was a kind of 'religious capital . . . without civic or political rival'; and this could not be without its impact on the spiritual mood of the people.

In the fifth century BC, there were new waves of returnees to Jerusalem from Babylon, the grand-children and great-grandchildren of the first exiles, and the ones who had most impact on the rebuilding of the city were those who were led by Ezra and Nehemiah. Nehemiah arrived with the Persian monarch's appointment as governor, and he and his fellow Jews promptly began, as their first task, to rebuild the walls of Jerusalem. The detailed account of their construction of the walls appears in the biblical Book of Nehemiah and tells that they followed the courses of the old ramparts which had been destroyed by Nebuchadnezzar. Destruction had been heaviest along the eastern and northern walls, which had to be rebuilt from the foundations, whereas work on other sections was largely reconstruction. At one point in his report on the restoration, Nehemiah says that 'they fortified Jerusalem unto the broad wall' (Nehemiah

3:8). It is Prof. Avigad's opinion that the portion of the seventh-century BC western city wall which he discovered in his excavations in the Jewish Quarter may well be part of this 'broad wall' referred to by Nehemiah. It is indeed unusually thick, more than 21 feet, and the section recently unearthed is more than 80 feet long and preserved to a height of 3 to 9 feet. The foundations were built on bedrock.

The Persian period (537–332 BC) ended with the conquest by Alexander the Great, and Jerusalem came under Hellenistic rule, first by the Ptolemies (up to 198 BC) and then by the Seleucids (198–167 BC). Little is known of the physical development of Jerusalem during these centuries. But the records are again abundant following the successful Jewish revolt in the year 167 BC headed by the Hasmoneans (the Maccabees) against the repressive Seleucid monarch Antiochus IV Epiphanes. Under the Hasmonean dynasty (167–63 BC) Jerusalem thrived, a reflection of the growing prosperity of the country which, at the beginning of the first century BC, almost reached the dimensions of the state achieved by David and Solomon. After cleansing and rededicating the Temple which had been desecrated by Antiochus (commemorated to this day by Jews everywhere in the Festival of Hannukah), the Hasmoneans fortified the Temple area and constructed a fort, called the Baris, at its north-western corner, built a royal palace and other handsome structures in the 'Upper City' – part of which is today's Jewish Quarter – and strengthened the city walls. The three rock-cut monuments in the Kidron Valley (erroneously called the Tombs of Absalom, St James and Zachariah) just below the south-east corner of the Temple Compound, which are still a familiar Jerusalem sight, may also belong to the Hasmonean period.

The Roman conquest under Pompey in 63 BC was followed by twenty-three years of Jewish rebellion against the occupiers, and, indeed, in the year 40 BC the last of the Hasmoneans, Mattathias Antigonus, ascended the throne. But success was brief. In 37

BC Herod, grandson of an Idumaean convert to Judaism and son of a leading counsellor at the Jewish court in earlier years, was able to secure massive Roman military support, overthrow the Hasmonean monarch, and become, as a vassal of Rome, the king of Judea. Though cruel and self-seeking, and hated by his Jewish subjects as a renegade who fawned on imperial Rome, Herod was an outstanding organiser with a remarkable talent and passion for building.

He built a magnificent royal palace, at the north-west corner of the 'Upper City', close to today's Jaffa Gate. At the northern end of the palace he constructed three huge towers, and the masonry of one of them, the Tower of Phasael, may still be seen just inside the Jaffa Gate. Herod had built so well that after his death his palace became successively the residence of the Roman procurators when they visited Jerusalem and a stronghold of the Jewish resisters in their final battle against the Romans in AD 70. The towers became the castle of the Byzantines, the fortress of the Moslems, the 'Tower of David' of the crusaders, and the Turkish citadel right up to our own times. Today it is variously called the Citadel and the Tower of David (though it has no Davidic connection).

At the north-west corner of the Temple Compound, Herod replaced the Hasmonean Baris with a rebuilt and enlarged castle which he named the Antonia Fortress in honour of Mark Antony. Parts of it may still be seen. According to Christian tradition, the trial of Jesus and the judgement by Pontius Pilate took place in the Antonia Fortress and the First Station of the Cross at the beginning of the Via Dolorosa is therefore located on its site (inside the Old City about 150 yards from the Lions' Gate).

Herod raised many other buildings in Jerusalem. But the pride of them all was his repair and reconstruction of the Temple, which had remained virtually unaltered for some 500 years. Herod's action was clearly a gesture of appeasement to his hostile Jewish subjects. Much of his magnificent masonry is still intact today. The ground plan of the Temple proper was the

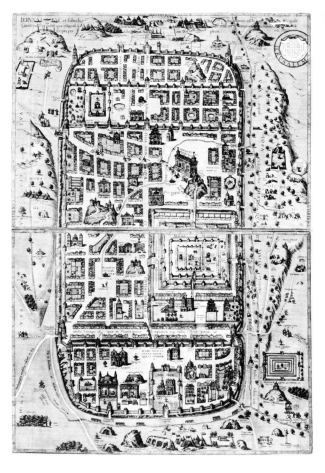

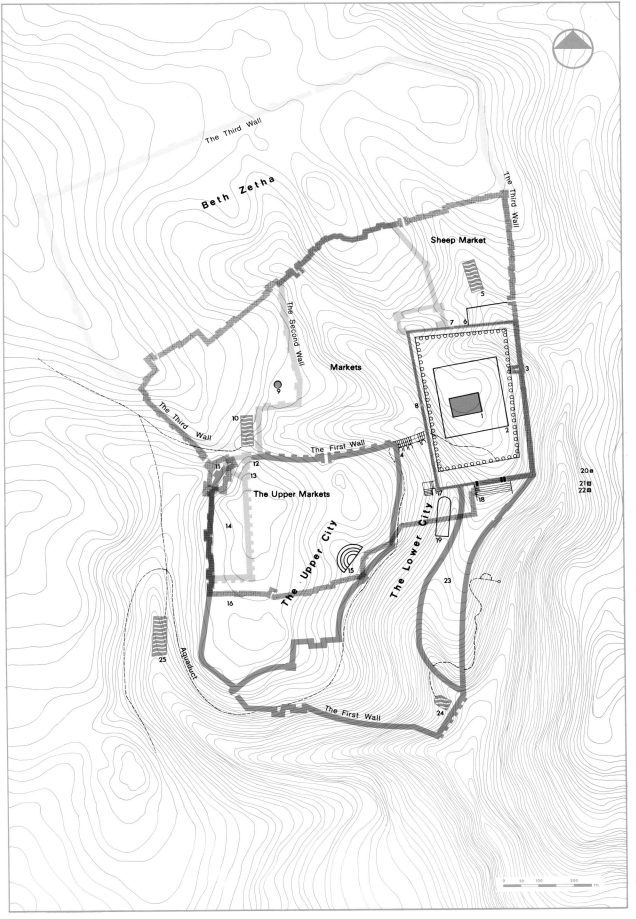

1 The Temple
2 The Balustrade
3 Gate of Susa
4 Wilson's Arch
5 The Sheep Pool
6 Pool of Israel
7 Tadi Gate
8 Warren's Gate
9 Golgotha Hill
10 Tower Pool
11 Tower of Phasael
12 Tower of Hippicus
13 Tower of Mariamne
14 Herod's Palace
15 Theatre
16 Palace of the High Priest
17 Robinson's Arch
18 Gates of Hulda
19 Hippodrome
20 Absalom's Pillar
21 Tomb of the Priestly Family of
   Hezir (Tomb of St James)
22 Pyramid of Zachariah
23 Palaces of the Kings
   of Adiabene
24 Siloam Pool
25 The Serpent's Pool

same as before, but he doubled its height and greatly amplified the porch so that the building seemed to soar. The impression was heightened by its huge colonnaded and walled courts. To provide an appropriate base for this immense architectural enterprise, he built a formidable platform, a great rectangular esplanade supported by substructures and great buttress walls rising from the ravines bounding the Temple Mount. The Western Wall (called by Christians the 'Wailing Wall'), with its massive Herodian stones, is one of these walls.

Since the Six Day War, additional Herodian structures in the vicinity of the Temple Compound have been brought to light at the excavations by Prof. Mazar. He rediscovered a street paved with well-shaped slabs of Jerusalem stone, which led up from the Tyropoeon Valley to the Double Gate (one of the 'Gates of Hulda') in the southern wall of the Temple Compound. Adjoining it was a broad plaza, also Herodian. In digging down to this street, the scholars exposed ten lower courses of the Herodian southern wall. The skewback of a Herodian arch just south of the Western Wall had been discovered by Robinson in the last century and has been known since then as Robinson's Arch. Mazar unearthed the foundation of the other extremity of this arch. Wilson's Arch, just north of the Western Wall, has recently been cleared of debris and it now stands exposed, a complete arch in a perfect state of preservation, the huge Herodian stones immaculately laid to form a flawless curve. Herod had built it to support the bridge leading from the 'Upper City' to the Temple Mount. Mazar's latest Herodian discovery (July 1971) is a staircase of monumental dimensions — some 350 feet broad — which led up to the Double and Triple Gates, the main entry for the populace to the Temple Compound.

Under Herod and his successors, the area of Jerusalem was steadily enlarged, and scholars estimate that its population may well have exceeded 150,000.

The next important contribution to Jerusalem's structures came in the years AD 41–44, when king Agrippa constructed a new city wall, known as the Third Wall (the first was probably built by the Hasmoneans and the second by Herod) in the north designed to give protection to the new suburb of Bethzetha. Some archaeologists believe that it followed the course of today's northern wall of the Old City, but many more hold that it lay further north.

In the year AD 70, after the grim four-year War of the Jews against the Romans, Jerusalem fell to the Legions led by Titus. The Temple was destroyed and the city ravaged. In their current archaeological excavations both Mazar and Avigad have found evidence of Titus' destruction. In the kitchen of a Jewish house which had been set on fire by the Roman troops, Avigad found the remains of a young woman in the very position in which she had met her death. Mazar's discovery was along the southern wall of the Temple Compound. Lying on the paved Herodian street which he had uncovered were Herodian building stones and architectural fragments which had fallen from the top courses of the wall during the battle, and the force of the impact had cracked some of the paving slabs.

Tens of thousand's of Jews had fallen in the fighting or were later slaughtered, and the surviving Jews of Jerusalem were carried off into exile. However, the children and grandchildren of the Jewish survivors in the rest of the country renewed their resistance, and in AD 132, led by Bar-Kokhba, they regained their independence. But this lasted only three years. The Roman emperor Hadrian brought in a considerable force, overwhelmed Bar-Kokhba and put an end to Jewish rule.

It was Hadrian's object to eradicate the name and memory of Jewish Jerusalem, and he accordingly sought to wipe out all physical trace of it and to erect upon its site a Roman city called Aelia Capitolina. (Aelius was Hadrian's family name and Capitoline Jupiter was the principal Roman god.) He put a plough to the locality and probably built his city in a smaller and more compact area, following the layout of a Roman camp. The design of Hadrian's city is of particular importance to the modern Jerusalem town-planner since several of its major features are followed by the Old City of today.

The courses of the walls are similar. As today, the southern Roman wall excluded the city of David, in the south-east, and Mount Zion, in the south-west. The west and east walls were bounded, as today, by the valleys of Kidron and Hinnom. There is a scholarly controversy over the north wall, but all agree that the remains of the arched entrance — which may be seen below the present Damascus Gate — belong to the Aelia Capitolina period.

Inside the city Hadrian laid down two main colonnaded roads, north–south and east–west, which bisected each other, terminated in gates and divided the city into four quarters (which became, in later ages, the Jewish, Moslem, Christian and Armenian quarters). Today's David Street and its extension, the Street of the Chain, follow the same line — between Jaffa Gate and the Temple Compound — as the Roman east–west road. The other Roman road ran roughly between today's Damascus and Zion gates. Near their intersection stood the Forum; it is today's Muristan bazaar.

Hadrian also built an aqueduct, a theatre and public baths, and to destroy, as he hoped, Jewish associations with Jerusalem, he built a temple to Jupiter on the site of the ancient Jewish Temple with an equestrian statue of himself in front of it. Jews were rigidly banned, on penalty of death, from entering or even approaching within sight of the city. (Only two centuries later was the ban slightly eased, the Jews

*Relief carved on a crocodile bone showing
the capture of Jerusalem by the Romans*

being permitted to visit the site of the Temple
one day in the year, the Ninth of Av, and mourn over
its ruins; and only in the fifth century was the general
prohibition lifted.)

Despite the considerable scope of Hadrian's building
activity, Jerusalem for the two centuries of its existence as Aelia Capitolina was a small, insignificant,
provincial town — its only period of insignificance
throughout its three thousand years of recorded
history — of interest only to the Jews, who were not
allowed to set foot in it, and to Christians, who began
to visit and live near the sites where Jesus had
preached, lived and died. Only in the fourth century,
with the emergence of Emperor Constantine and his
adoption of Christianity, were the name and stature of
Jerusalem restored. Henceforth, it was to become for
Christians what it had been for the Jews for thirteen
centuries: their Holy City. With it came many structural
additions.

1   Tombs
2   The Sheep Pool
3   Triumphal Arch
4   Temple of Jupiter
5   Hadrianus Statue
6   The Perforated Stone
7   Baths
8   Inscription
9   Tetranymphon
10 Spring
11 Baths
12 Theatre
13 Inscription
14 Cardo
15 Decumanus
16 Praetorium
17 Tetrapylon
18 Inscription
19 Tower Pool
20 Aphrodite Temple
21 Column
22 Inscription

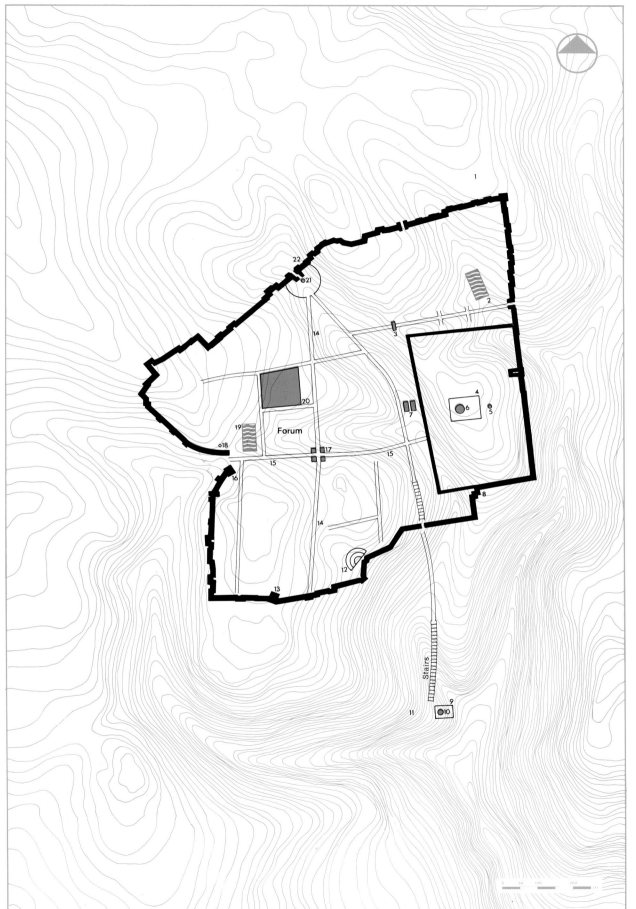

Jerusalem during the Byzantine Period, 324–638

opposite *The 6th-century mosaic map of Jerusalem found at Madeba in 1897. See the column (archway) along the main roads from the Damascus Gate*

Constantine's mother, Queen Helena, visited the Holy Land in 326, and it was she who determined the locations of the crucifixion and burial of Jesus and the the sites of other events associated with his final days. Upon these sites Constantine erected appropriate shrines, the most important of which was the Church of the Holy Sepulchre, which is preserved – in part – to this day, though there were numerous reconstructions. The other outstanding Constantinian basilica in Jerusalem was the Church of Eleona on the Mount of Olives, the remains of which were discovered during archaeological excavations in 1910. (They lie beneath today's new Basilica of the Sacred Heart.) The original Church of the Ascension, also on the Mount of Olives, was constructed some fifty years after the death of Helena. In the following two centuries, with the growing Christian community and the increasing number of pilgrims, monks and nuns, the city began to abound with monasteries, convents, hospices and additional churches.

The architectural state of Jerusalem in the latter part of the sixth century may be seen in the mosaic map discovered in 1897 in the ruins of a church at Madeba, in Jordan, east of the Dead Sea. The map shows that by now the city walls had been extended in the south-west to take in Mount Zion with its church and palace. (It is today the site of the Dormition Abbey, as well as the building containing the traditional Tomb of David and the Coenaculum, traditional site of the Last Supper.) Prominently featured are the Church of the Holy Sepulchre, its entrance flanked by Hadrian's colonnaded north-south street, a gate commanding a broad plaza on the site of today's Damascus Gate; and two towers close by the west gate of the city, the Jaffa Gate of today. These were two of Herod's three original towers built at the northern end of his palace-citadel, and one of them is evidently Phasael, whose base is preserved today on the 'Tower of David'. Grouped between the outstanding structures in this Madeba mosaic are thick clusters of smaller churches and hospices, and though it is natural that Christian buildings should be given prominence in the decorative floor of a

church, it is evident that they were the outstanding features of Byzantine Jerusalem.

Byzantine rule ended briefly in 614, when Jerusalem fell to the Persians, and many churches and other buildings were destroyed. But the city was regained – also briefly – in 629, and rebuilding work was under way when, in 638, the Moslem forces, under Caliph Omar, reached and besieged Jerusalem and the Christians surrendered without a struggle.

Jerusalem during the Moslem Period, 638–1099

Omar was careful not to harm Jerusalem because of the association of the Temple site – the traditional rock of Mount Moriah – with a dream of Mohammed. The caliph asked to be taken to the Temple Compound and was angered to find that the Byzantines had turned it into a refuse dump. He had it cleared and erected a wooden mosque on the site believed to be the place where Abraham was commanded to sacrifice his son Isaac. Some fifty years later, the caliph Abd el-Malik built the great shrine on this site – the Dome of the Rock. It underwent many restorations in the succeeding centuries, and there were several decorative additions; but it is basically the same magnificent octagonal building, crowned by a gilded dome, as conceived by its creators, and it remains the outstanding landmark of Jerusalem.

In later centuries, as various Moslem rulers sought to decorate the huge Herodian Jewish Temple platform which Islam had taken over and renamed the Haram esh-Sharif (Noble Sanctuary), small minarets, towers and fountains were added, as were broad flights of steps leading up to this spacious plaza from all sides, topped by slender arches. At its southern end, the silver-domed Mosque of El-Aksa was constructed early in the eighth century, but it suffered great destruction by earthquake and was the subject of frequent reconstruction. Of the original building, only a few pillars of a colonnade remain.

Jerusalem was never the capital of the Arab empire, and no Arab leader was ever inspired to make it so. Abd el-Malik built the Dome of the Rock for political and economic reasons in order to divert the pilgrimage from Mecca, with whose rulers he was in conflict. He did not succeed completely; but the grandeur of his building was such that in the course of time Jerusalem became the third holy city of Islam. However, its sacredness to Jews and Christians was recognised. Jews were allowed to return, and both they and Christians were tolerated and allowed control of their communal affairs. Their fortunes rose and fell at the whim of the successive caliphs of the different dynasties. By and large there was a good deal of construction during the Moslem period, though the broad design of Jerusalem remained unchanged.

A good tenth-century glimpse of the city is to be found in the work of the Moslem geographer Mukaddasi, who wrote: 'Among provincial towns, none is larger than Jerusalem . . . The buildings of the Holy City are of stone, and you will find nowhere finer or more solid constructions . . . The markets are clean, the mosque is of the largest and nowhere are holy places more numerous.'

It was under the harsh Fatimid Caliph Al-Hakim that Jerusalem suffered havoc. He banned Jewish and Christian pilgrimage and ordered the destruction of churches and synagogues throughout the empire. It was at this time that the Church of the Holy Sepulchre was destroyed, and this is said to have done more than any other single act of Moslem vandalism to awaken the idea in the Christian world of possible military action against Islamic rule in Palestine. However, the churches were allowed to be reconstructed and pilgrimage was resumed after the death of Al-Hakim. But in 1071 Jerusalem came under the control of the Seljuk Turks, who pillaged the city and persecuted both Christians and Jews. It was their maltreatment of the Christians which spurred the Christian counter-offensive. On 15 July 1099 the First Crusade captured Jerusalem.

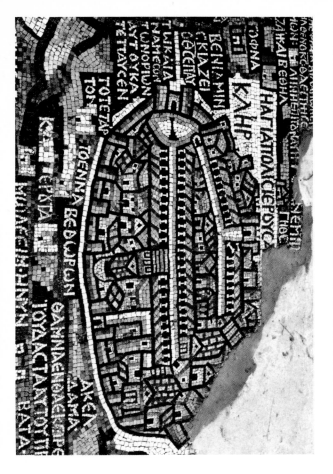

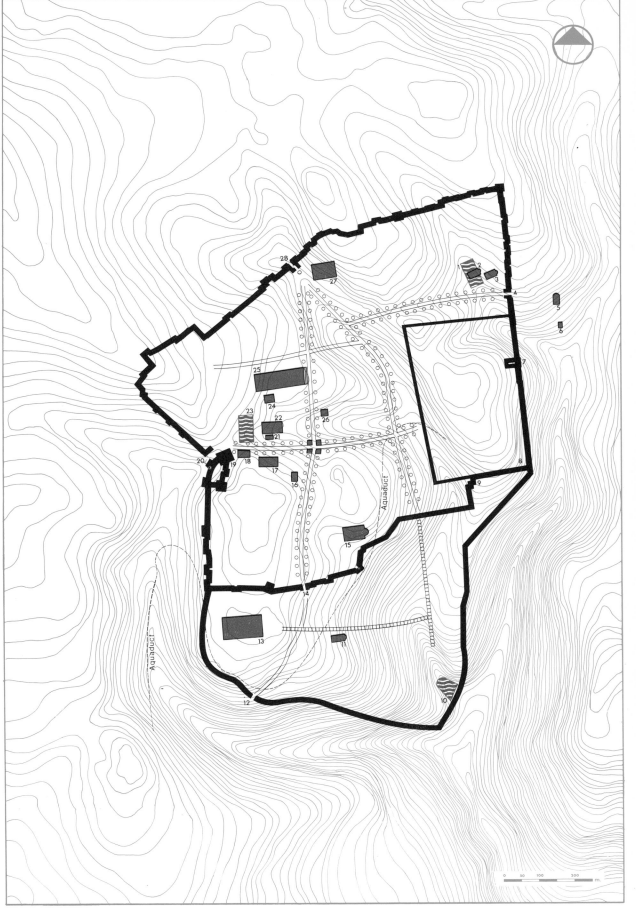

1   Pool of Bethesda
2   Church of the Paralytic
3   St Mary's Birth
4   The Jericho Gate
5   Tomb of the Virgin
6   Gethsemane
7   Golden Gate
8   The Pinnacle
9   Double Gate
10 The Pool
11 St Peter
12 Tekoa Gate
13 Holy Zion
14 Zion Gate
15 Nea
16 Syrian Convent
17 Iberian Convent
18 St Saba Convent
19 David's Tower
20 David's Gate
21 St John
22 Greek Monastery
23 Pool of the Patriarch
24 Baptisterium
25 Holy Sepulchre
26 Aged Asylum
27 Palace of Eudoxia
28 St Stephan's Gate

The Crusader Kingdom, 1099–1187

opposite *An early (1170) crusader map of Jerusalem*

After a forty-day siege, the crusaders succeeded in bridging the north wall of the city — near the present Herod's Gate, where the wall is lowest — from the top of a siege tower and simultaneously, operating from Mount Zion, in taking the southern wall by the same means. The Saracen army surrendered and the crusaders went on a rampage through Jerusalem, slaughtering Jews and Moslems alike (the Christian community had departed) and destroying the synagogues and some mosques, but taking over the Dome of the Rock and the Mosque of El-Aksa for Christian use. Jersalem became the Crusader kingdom, which was to last, with long interruptions, for two hundred years.

The shape of the city was much the same as that of Aelia Capitolina, with Mount Zion again outside the walls. (The walls of Mount Zion were probably destroyed by Al-Hakim.) These followed roughly the courses of today's Old City walls. There was a feverish drive to erect ecclesiastical buildings of every kind — churches and hospices, convents and monasteries and residences for the clergy. The Church of the Holy Sepulchre received prime attention. It was completely rebuilt and given the outline that exists in large part today. Constantine's rectangular edifice was changed into the form of a cross, and Golgotha, the sepulchre and associate shrines were united under a single roof. Only the rotunda of the sepulchre followed Constantine's design and rose on the original foundations. Further chapels and cloisters were added.

Most of the Christian structures were built in the 'Patriarch's Quarter' — today's Christian Quarter — in the north-west, and in the 'Armenian Quarter', as it is still called, in the south-west. But crusader establishments were also erected in the south-east quarter, today's Jewish Quarter, and in the north-east, then known as 'Jewry' and also as the 'Syrian Quarter' and today's Moslem Quarter. The most notable church built there was the Church of St Anne, preserved to this day.

The Temple Mount was converted into a Christian religious centre by the Order of Knights Templar. The Dome of the Rock became their central church and the Mosque of El-Aksa their headquarters. (El-Aksa was considered to have been the site of the royal palace built by King Solomon, just south of the Temple, and since the vaults beneath the mosque were used as stables by the knights, they were called the 'Stables of Solomon'. They are intact to this day, and they are still known by this name; but they are not Solomonic. They were built to support this southern section of the Temple esplanade.) South of the Citadel the palace of the king and garrison headquarters were built.

Despite the considerable building boom, crusader Jerusalem failed to attract a sizeable permanent Christian settlement. It was a city occupied by troops, ecclesiastics, transient pilgrims and the men and women who served them. One pilgrim record describes the gates, streets and colourful bazaars of the crusader city: 'The Gate of David [today's Jaffa Gate] is towards the west . . .' Inside this gate was David Street, as it is still called, and 'when you come to the Exchange where David Street ends there is a street called Mount Zion Street, for it goes straight to Mount Zion; and on the left of the Exchange is a covered street, vaulted over, called the Street of Herbs, where they sell all the herbs and all the fruits of the city and spices. At the top of this street is a place where they sell fish. And behind the market where they sell the fish is a very large place on the left hand where cheese, chickens and eggs are sold. On the right hand of this market are the shops of the Syrian goldworkers . . . Before the Exchange, close to the Street of Herbs, is a street which they call Mal-quisinat. In this street they cooked food for the pilgrims . . .' This description, written eight hundred years ago, evokes the lively and colourful mood of the Old City bazaars of today. Indeed, some of the vaulted market-alleys of that period still stand.

The crusaders lost Jerusalem in 1187, less than three months after the decisive defeat of their armies in the battle at the Horns of Hittin at the hands of an Armenian Kurd of Moslem faith, the brilliant military and political leader Saladin (Salah ad-Din). However, they retained a coastal stronghold in the north, based on Acre, and in 1229, through diplomacy, they were given control of Jerusalem, but were again flung out in 1244. That was the end of Christian rule in Jerusalem until the British Mandatory period seven centuries later. (Crusader rule in the north of the country came to an end in 1291.)

Saladin's first step in Jerusalem was to arrange for the Dome of the Rock and the Mosque of El-Aksa to be purified and restored from Christian to Moslem places of worship. He also lifted the crusader ban on Jewish settlement in the Holy City. He then returned to Damascus. For all its sanctity, Jerusalem, to Moslem Saladin, was no more than a provincial centre.

In 1249 the Ayyubid Caliphate was overthrown by the Mamelukes, Turkish and Circassian professional soldiers who had been in the service of the caliphs and who suddenly seized control from their former masters. For the next 267 years, Jerusalem was to be administered by a governor appointed by the Mameluke sultan.

In the early years of their administration, the Mamelukes, who built much and were patrons of the arts, also applied part of their architectural programme to Jerusalem. They rebuilt the walls of the city, which had been allowed to fall into disrepair, and a 1321 map shows that Mount Zion was once again included within the walls. They reconstructed the Citadel, giving it the form with which we are familiar today. They expanded the city's water supply, repaired an aqueduct which brought water from the Hebron Hills and constructed additional pools. Several churches were converted into mosques, the most notable of which was the Church of St Anne. (It was restored to the Christians in the nineteenth century.)

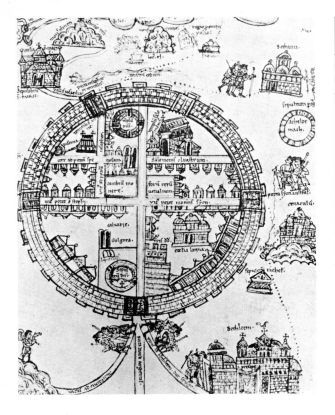

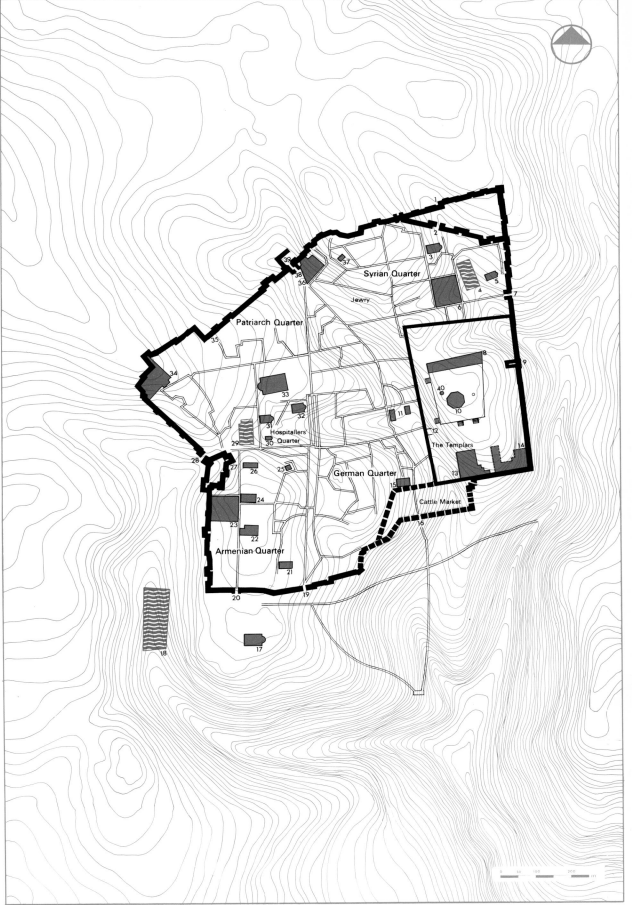

1   Breach of 1099
2   Postern of St Magdalena
3   St Magdalena
4   Pools
5   St Anne
6   Pilatus House
7   Gate of Jehoshaphat
8   The Temple Convent
9   Golden Gate
10 Templum Domini
11 Baths
12 Beautiful Gate
13 Templum Salomonis
14 Templar Stables
15 St Mary of the Germans
16 Postern of the Tanners
17 St Mary of Mount Zion
18 Germain's Pool
19 Zion Gate
20 Belcaire Postern
21 Anna's House
22 St James
23 The Royal Palace
24 St Thomas
25 Syrian Monastery
26 St James
27 David's Tower
28 David's Gate
29 Pool of the Patriarch
30 St John
31 St Mary La-Granda
32 St Mary La-Latina
33 Holy Sepulchre
34 Tancred's Tower
35 Postern of St Lazare
36 Palace of La-Latina
37 St Agnes
38 St Stephan's Gate
39 St Abraham
40 Baptisterium

Jerusalem under the Mamelukes, 1250–1517

The main Mameluke beautification work was applied to Moslem buildings. They built handsome *madrassahs*—a combination of mosque and religious school in the hope that Jerusalem might become an important centre of Moslem learning; but though it produced a number of pious scholars, Jerusalem never became the seat or even a centre of Islamic theology. The Haram esh-Sharif was adorned with fountains, arches and minarets, and the graceful arcades which still stand at the top of the steps leading up to the gracious plaza belong to the early Mameluke period.

Unlike the crusaders, the Mamelukes were, on the whole, tolerant of other religions, and Christians and Jews were allowed freedom of worship, though they were subjected to certain restrictions. The Jews quickly took advantage of their regained freedom, and soon there was once again a Jewish community in the city. Among the Jews who arrived in Jerusalem during this immediate post-crusader period were rabbis and scholars, the most renowned of whom was the great thirteenth-century sage from Spain, Rabbi Moshe ben Nachman, better known as Nachmanides, who came to settle in 1267. He established a centre of Jewish learning and reconstructed a synagogue which bore his name ever after. (This synagogue was confiscated by the Moslems in subsequent centuries and later used as a factory. Only now, after the Six Day War, has it been repaired, renovated and restored as a synagogue.) The community grew and engaged in handicrafts and commerce, but its main preoccupation was with Talmudic study. The 1331 record of a pilgrim notes that of the Jewish scholars who had settled in Jerusalem, 'some are devoted to science, [such] as medicine, astronomy, and mathematics'.

The Jews in early times chose a burial site as close as possible to the Temple. 'At the foot of the slope of the Temple Mount are Jewish graves', a noted rabbi reported at the end of the fifteenth century, and when these were filled up, following the growth in the Jewish community, 'the new ones [graves] are at the foot of the Mount of Olives, and the valley [of Kidron] runs between the graveyards'. Over the centuries, the Jewish cemetery crept right up the slope of the Mount of Olives and became the most revered burial site of Jewry. (The rabbi we quoted died in 1510 and was buried there.) This ancient Jewish cemetery was destroyed by the Jordanians during their 1948–67 occupation, and only after the Six Day War were the smashed tombstones repaired or replaced and other marks of vandalism removed.

Jerusalem declined in the final century of Mameluke rule, smitten by governmental indifference with its consequent maladministration, as well as by natural disaster — earthquake, famine and plague. The population became impoverished and dwindled from 40,000 to 10,000; buildings and the city walls fell into ruin. This was also a reflection of a weakening Mameluke authority, and in the closing days of 1516, Mameluke dominion over Jerusalem was swept away by the Ottoman Turks. For the next four hundred years, Jerusalem was to remain part of the Ottoman Empire.

A 16th-century map of Jerusalem, the first topographically accurate representation of the city

1 Mad. Salahiya
2 Mad. Muazzamiya
3 Mad. Sallamiya
4 Mad. Amminiya
5 Mad. Malikiya
6 Mad. Jawiliya
7 Mad. Keramiya
8 Mad. Fahariza
9 Mad. Faresiya
10 Mad. Issardiya
11 Mad. Manjukiah
12 Ribat Alla ed-Din el Basiri
13 Turbat es-Sit
14 Ribat Bayram Tashwish
    (Resasiya)
15 Dar es-Sit
16 Mad. Hatunia
17 Hammam el Ein
18 Gate of the Cotton
    Merchants
19 Mad. el Ut-maniya
20 Mad. Ashrafiya
21 Kait-Bey's Sabil
22 Minaret
23 Tur. Jaligiya
24 Mad. Tankiziya
25 Tur. Jaligiya
26 Mad. Taziya
27 Mad. Luluiya
28 Zawiya Kiramiya
29 Mad. Baddariya
30 Minaret of Ommariya
31 Khankat Salahiya
32 Khan es-Sultan
33 Mad. Tashtamuriya
34 Tur. Barakat Han
35 El Kas
36 The Karaite Synagogue
37 Rambam Synagogue
38 Sultan's Pool

Buildings from Early Arabic Period
A Dome of the Rock
B Dome of the Chain
C El-Aksa Mosque

Mad.—Madrassa—School
Tur.—Turbat—Mausoleum
Khan—Traders' Inn
Khanka—Convent
Sabil—Drinking Place
Ribat—Pilgrims' Hostel

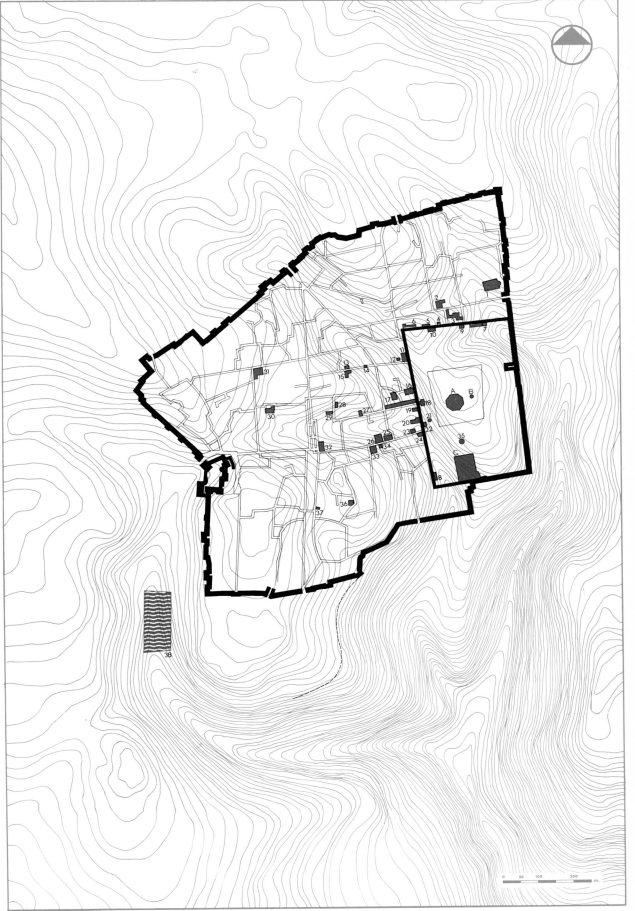

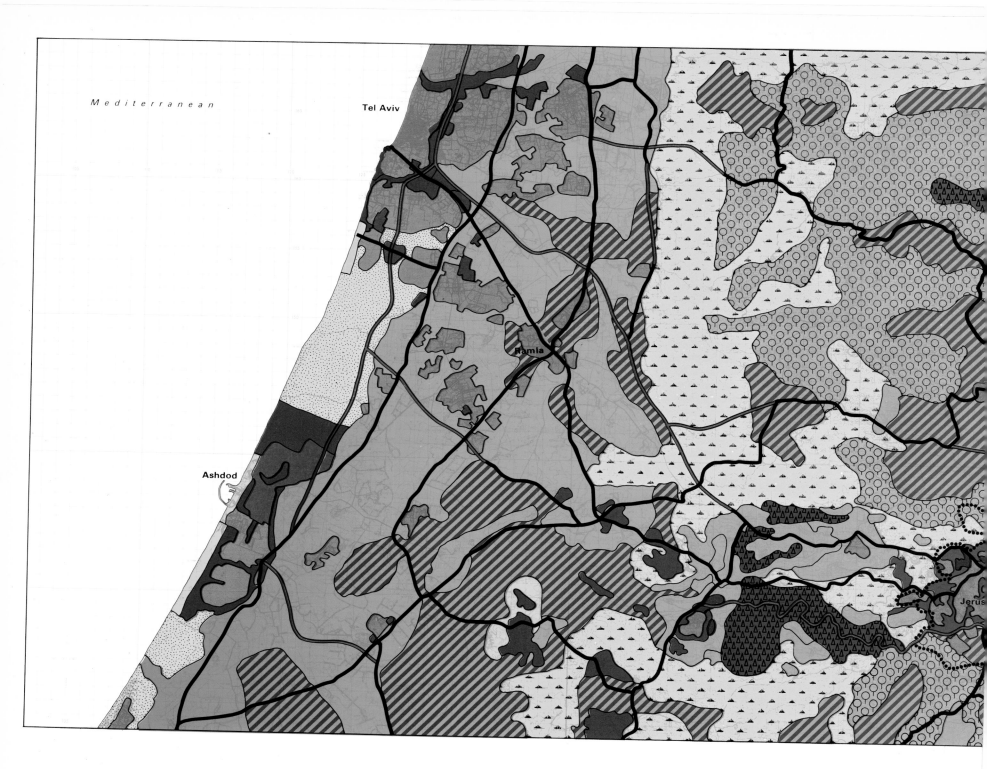

Mediterranean

Tel Aviv

Ramla

Ashdod

Jerus

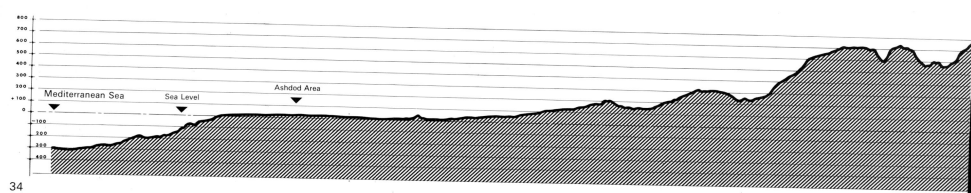

800
700
600
500
400
300
200
+100
0
−100
200
300
400

Mediterranean Sea

Sea Level

Ashdod Area

The Changing Landscape
Jerusalem between the Mediterranean and the Dead Sea

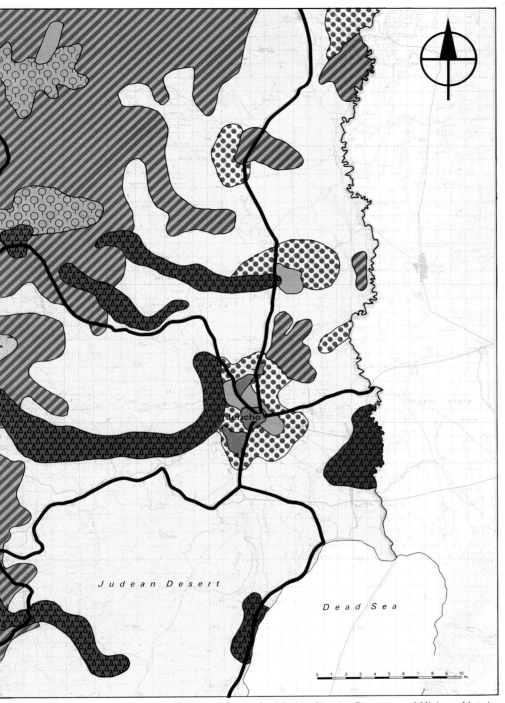

Map based on data furnished by Planning Department of Ministry of Interior

----------	Municipal Boundary
━━━━━	Existing Road
═════	Proposed Road
�▓▓▓	Built-up Area
███	Industrial Zone
░░░	Bathing Beach
▓▓▓	Public Open Space
▲▲▲	National Park and Nature Reserve
▒▒▒	Irrigated Farm Land
▨▨▨	Unirrigated Farm Land
⦾⦾⦾	Orchards
●●●	Single Crop Plantation
∴∴∴	Pasture
⣿⣿⣿	Sand Dune

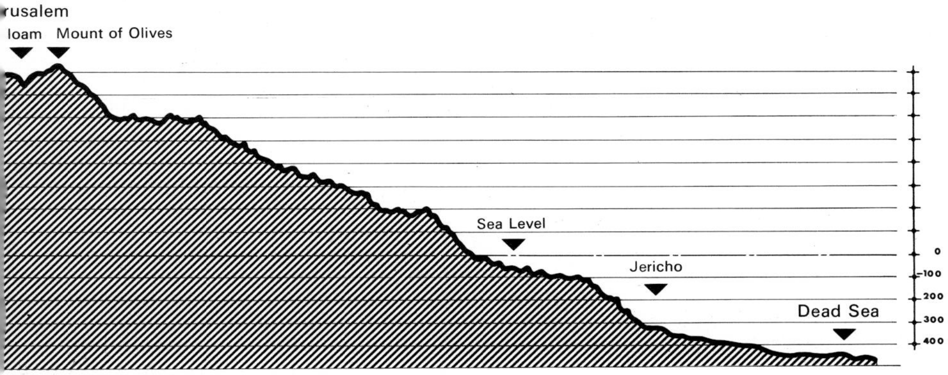

Cross-Section from Mediterranean to Dead Sea

*Landscape east of Jerusalem — the Judean
Desert*
opposite *Aerial view of the Western
approaches to Jerusalem*

View from the Mount of Olives onto the
eastern slopes surrounding the Old City.
In the foreground are the terraced and partly
planted slopes and the graveyards of ancient
cemeteries adjoining the City Wall

Jerusalem – View from the West

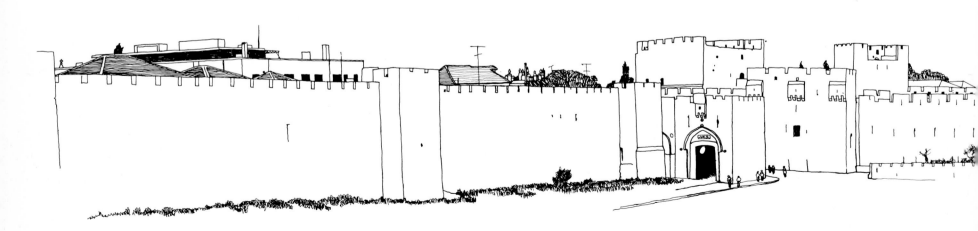

Perspective of West Wall

View from the North

*Perspective of North Wall with New Gate
at right, Damascus Gate in centre and Herod's
Gate at left*

Chapter 4   The Walls and Gates of Jerusalem

The Walls and Gates
of Jerusalem

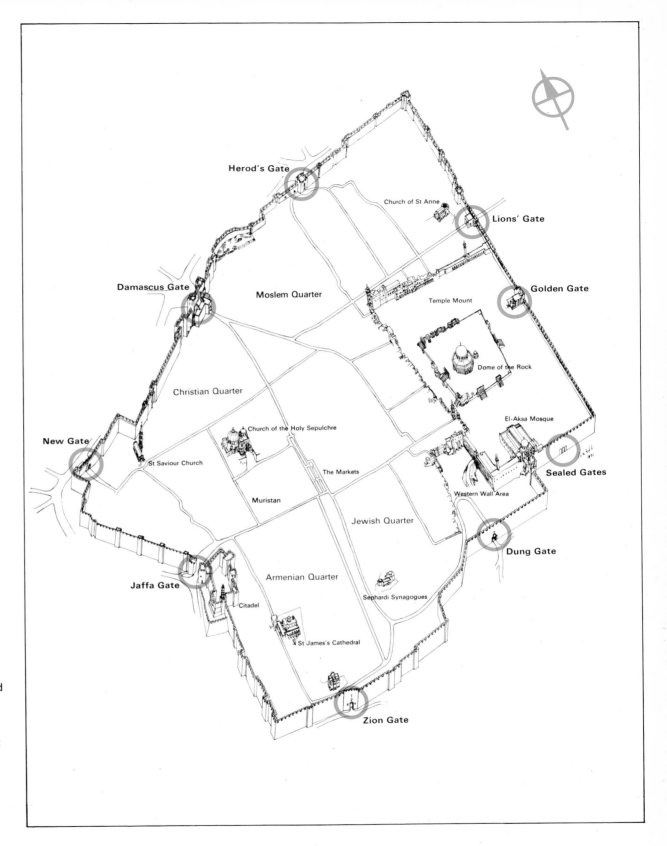

In their present course and shape, the walls and gates of Jerusalem are, as we have seen, those built by Suleiman the Magnificent, partly on remains from earlier epochs. Some of the huge stone masonry dates back to the period of the Second Temple. From inscriptions on the gates and towers, it appears that Suleiman's wall construction was completed in four years, from 1537 to 1541.

The walls enclose the Old City and are some 4 kilometres in length, ranging in height between 8 and 14 metres. Though the alignment of the walls does not follow natural topography, it is dictated by the earlier alignment traced by the Roman city plan. Their thickness, height and the nature of their construction vary according to the topography, the ground and the special fortification needs at the time of their foundation.

There are eleven gates which pierce the walls at irregular intervals. Four of them have been sealed for centuries. Seven now give access to the Old City, and most of them are sited at the natural extension of the main roads and paths leading to the city from the outside. These gates differ greatly in size and design, but all (except the Damascus Gate) originally followed the common basic plan of the indirect L-shaped entry, so that one entered a high vaulted chamber and then turned (left) and out through a second entranceway into the city. (The Damascus Gate had a more indirect entry, shaped like the Hebrew letter *lamed* [ל], with two turns, left and right, before reaching the inner entranceway.) This staggered entry was an old defence device to give advantage to the guards protecting the gate and to hinder the invader. A direct entry would make it more vulnerable to attack.

Ottoman Period

Mameluke Period

Herodian Period

*Section of south-eastern corner showing
different building periods of the Wall
opposite Architectural features typical of the
Wall*

48

Pinnacles   **Turrets**   **Windows**   **Rosettes**

49

Jaffa Gate

It will be recalled that the Old City is roughly square shaped. Its western wall, whose northernmost point adjoins the commercial quarters of the new city, rises steeply above the Valley of Hinnom and has a 120-degree angle break almost at its centre, near the Jaffa Gate. This is the only gate in this wall, and from time immemorial it offered the principal entrance to the Old City. Its name in Arabic is Bab el-Khalil, the Gate of Hebron, as the main road to Hebron started from this gate. (It was also called Jaffa Gate because the road to Jaffa and the coast started from there too.)

Jaffa Gate is in the form of a tower which projects forward from the wall, and its façade, which holds the arched entranceway topped by embrasures and stone turrets, is at right angles to the line of the wall and thus stands out very conspicuously. The arched entrance gives on to a vaulted chamber which is part of the L-shaped passageway leading through the tower into the city. Inside the city, close to the gate, is a small graveyard containing two tombs behind a wrought-iron fence. Buried there, according to legend, are Suleiman's architects, who were beheaded by the sultan when he discovered that they had left Mount Zion outside the walls. (They had no doubt done so for purely technical reasons. Architects beware!)

For centuries, the sole entry into the city from the west was through this tower of Jaffa Gate. In 1898, however, the Turkish sultan Abdul Hamid filled in a section of the moat between the gate and the nearby Citadel, which had been part of the ancient defensive system, in order to enable his friend, the German Kaiser Wilhelm II, to make an elaborate the-atrical entry into the Old City on horseback (thereby defying the ancient tradition for official visitors to the Holy City to enter on foot). Motor vehicles from the west now enter the Old City through this opening.

The Citadel has been a fortress of Jerusalem ever since Herod built his fortified Citadel on the site, protected by three huge towers. It was rebuilt many times, the latest constructions by the crusaders, the Mamelukes and the Ottomans. As we have observed earlier, several lower courses of the walls of Phasael, one of Herod's towers, may still be seen at the north-eastern tower of the Citadel, inside Jaffa Gate. They form the base of the later tower and are easily discernible by the size of their stones, similar to the monumental masonry of the Western Wall of the Temple Compound. It was probably this tower which in later centuries was given the popular but erroneous name of the Tower of David and became the symbolic landmark of the Old City.

The new pedestrian approach to the gate, bottom left, is at present under construction (see page 190)

Front Elevation

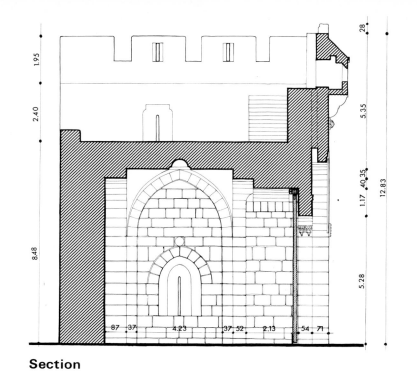

Section

Detail

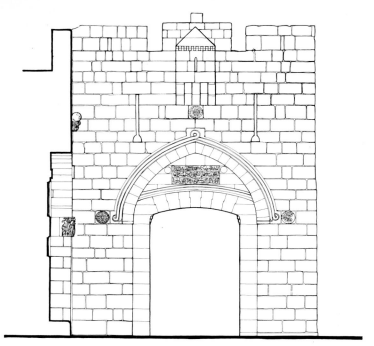

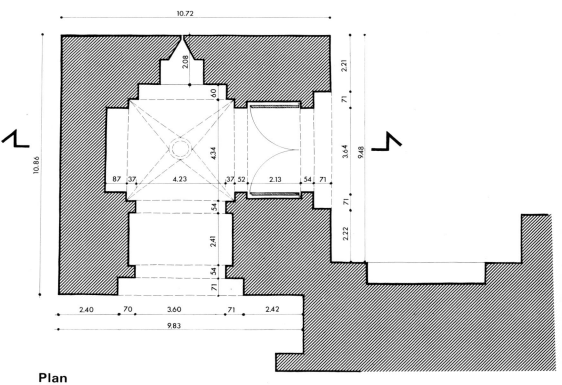

Plan

Damascus Gate

The northern wall of the city has three gates. The one near the north-west corner, and the least interesting of all, is the New Gate. It is little more than an opening in the wall — wide enough to take motor traffic — and it was constructed as recently as 1887 by Sultan Abdul Hamid to provide easy access to the Christian Quarter of the Old City from the developing new northern suburbs outside the walls. It still serves this purpose, though not very adequately, and its architecture is unexciting.

Mid-way along the northern wall is the Damascus Gate, the most massive and ornate of all Jerusalem's gates. Its central location in this wall made it the principal entrance to the Old City from the north, the road running off it leading to Shechem (Nablus) and on to Damascus, while the intersecting road which skirts the wall leads east to Jericho and the Dead Sea and west to the new suburbs of West Jerusalem.

The present Damascus Gate is the one which Suleiman rebuilt and which he may well have considered the pride of his wall structures. It is indeed one of the richest examples of early Ottoman architecture in the region, monumental yet graceful. Its walls are 16 metres high. Its arched portal is set in a broad façade flanked on each side by a great tower, and the entire building is topped by pinnacled battlements of such felicitous design that they serve as a counter-weight to the massive stone wall. The staggered entrance is handsomely vaulted, and after a left and right turn the passage-way opens onto the bazaar area of the Old City.

Though powerful looking, the Damascus Gate would seem to be more decorative than defensive. Above the portal, for example, are rows of bosses, the lower one adorned with reliefs of flowers and geometric patterns. They appear at first glance to be the protruding ends of binding columns running through the walls to strengthen the structure, which was a not uncommon architectural device in those days. But there are no such strengthening columns in this gate.

During archaeological excavations on this site in 1937, the remains of an ancient structure were discovered, consisting of typical Herodian masonry. Its huge stones — some weighing several tons — resemble those at the Western Wall. This archaeological stratum was 8 metres below the present level of the gate and had been covered by the debris of repetitive ruin over the centuries. The excavations also revealed that the Romans in the second century AD, in constructing Aelia Capitolina, had built their gate on this site upon the Herodian remains. Relics were also found of Byzantine repairs carried out in the fourth century. A heavy concrete bridge built during the Mandatory regime now spans the lower level of the antiquities to link the busy street outside the walls with the entrance to Damascus Gate.

Entrance bridge to Damascus Gate opposite *City rooftops behind the pinnacled façade of the Damascus Gate. In the foreground, gardens planted during the Jordanian administration*

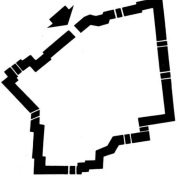

1

2

1　The new and the old. Below the present
　Damascus Gate are remnants of Herodian
　masonry and an arch considered by some
　archaeologists to have been built by
　Agrippa in the 1st century AD and
　incorporated in the 2nd-century AD
　structure by Hadrian
2　The soaring pinnacles of the Damascus
　Gate façade
3　The new entrance bridge above the
　archaeological moat
4　A 19th-century lithograph

3

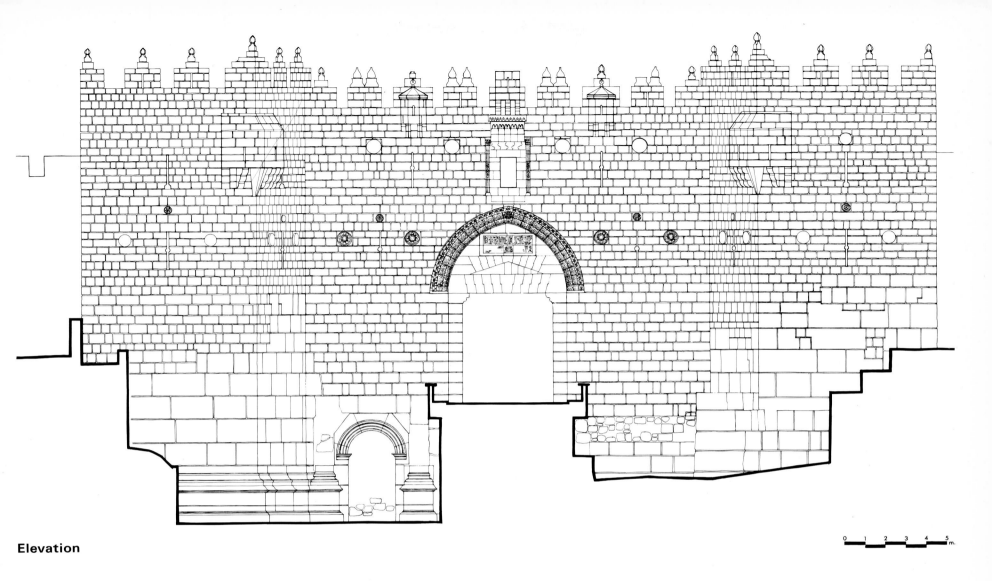

Elevation

4

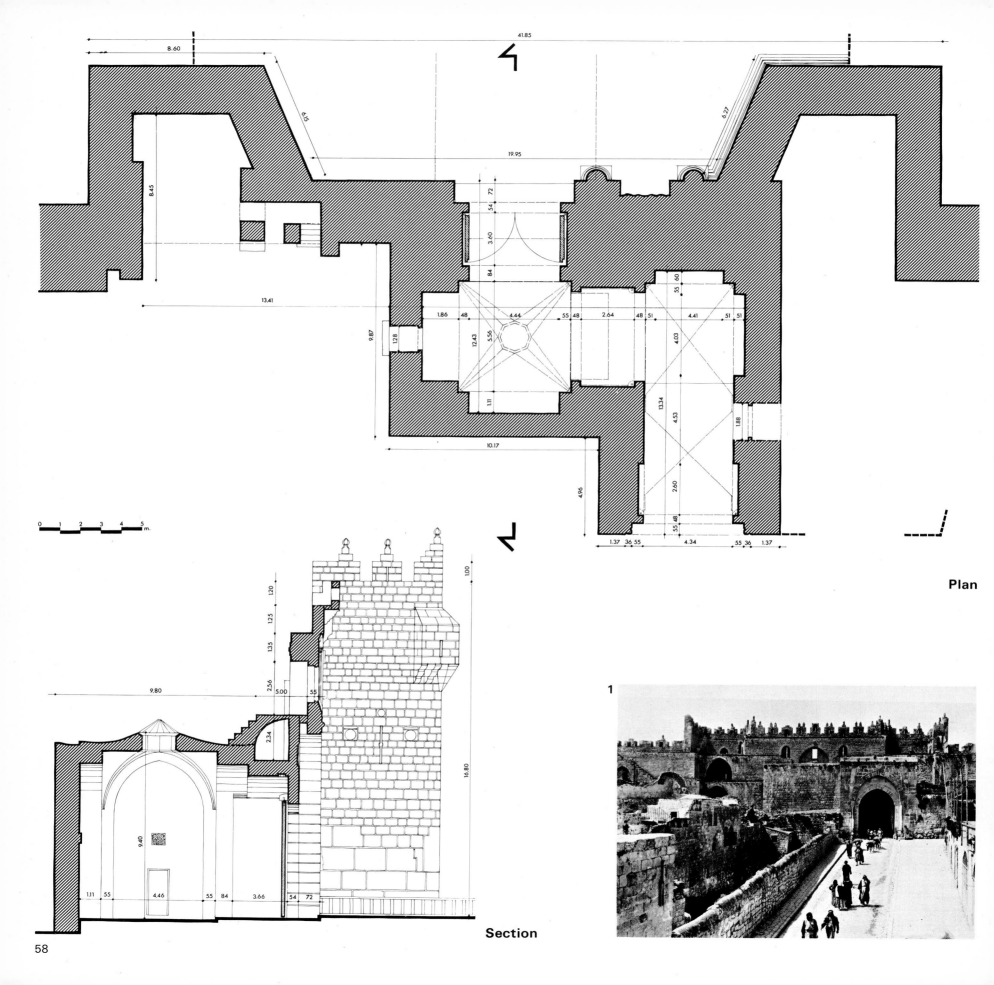

Plan

Section

1

58

1 *A 19th-century photograph showing the approach to the gate from inside the city*
2 *Steps leading from Damascus Gate towards the market*

Herod's Gate

The third gate in the northern wall is located near the north-east corner and leads directly into the Moslem Quarter of the Old City. This is Herod's Gate, so named by pilgrims who erroneously believed that it led to Herod's palace. It is also known in Arabic as the Flower Gate. It was close to this gate that men under the command of the crusader leader Godfrey de Bouillon succeeded in reaching the top of the wall from their siege tower and launching their final assault against the Saracens in 1099. (The impressive Rockefeller Museum, built in the nineteen-thirties opposite Herod's Gate, stands on the site of the crusader encampment.)

As does Jaffa Gate, Herod's Gate projects from the wall, like a jutting tower, and its original entranceway was in the sidewall of the tower at right-angles to the city wall. However, this entrance was later sealed because it was too narrow to admit wheeled traffic, mostly donkey-carts, and a new opening was made in the face of the tower, parallel to the city wall. This, incidentally, now gives direct entry into the Old City, instead of the original indirect L-shaped entry.

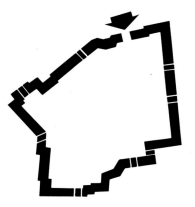

1 A view of Herod's Gate. The animals in this 1938 photograph are a timely reminder that in ancient times this gate was called the Sheep Gate
2 A decorative detail adorning the original entrance of the gate in the side-wall

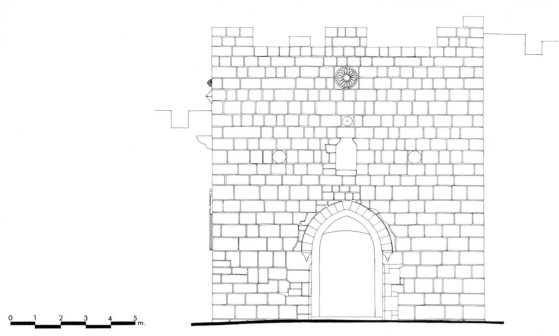

Elevation

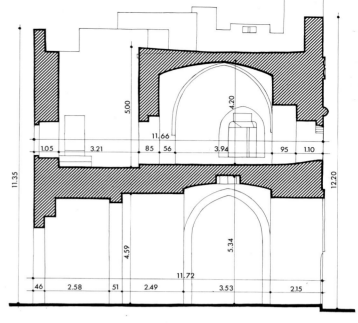

Section

2

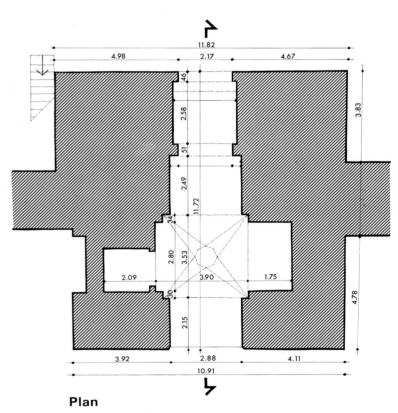

Plan

The Lions' Gate was
originally an L-shaped
structure, but was later
turned into a direct
entranceway to permit
the passage of wheeled
traffic

The Lions' Gate

The eastern wall, rising above the steep western bank
of the Kidron Valley, with its ancient cemetery and
tombstones, has two impressive gates, the Lions'
Gate, or St Stephen's Gate, which is open, and the
Golden Gate, which has been sealed for centuries.
The Lions' Gate is only a few yards north of the
northern wall of the Temple Compound and is the
gate closest to the First Station of the Cross in the
Via Dolorosa. Like Herod's Gate, it leads directly to
the Moslem Quarter. It also forms the main link between the Old City and some of the most revered
places in Christendom outside the walls, the Garden
of Gethsemane and other shrines on the slopes of the
Mount of Olives across the valley. Since the Crusades,
Christian pilgrims have called it St Stephen's Gate,
in the belief that the first Christian martyr was put
to death in the Kidron Valley just below.

The Lions' Gate is approached by a steep and narrow
uphill lane which runs off the Jericho road. The lane is
lined on either side by trees backed by high walls,
which make it seem even narrower; but as it nears the
top it broadens into a charming plaza, which serves as
a kind of forecourt to the gate and brings out the full
measure of its magnificence. It also lends an air of
quiet tranquillity to this entrance to the city, in
contrast to the bustling activity round the other gates.
This gate, as some others, had an indirect entry, but
during the British Mandate its back wall was removed
in order to enable vehicular traffic through. The arched
portal is set in a handsomely decorated façade, topped
by battlements and studded with stone carvings. The
most notable of these — which give the gate its
Hebrew name — are four lions, two on either side of
the portal. There is a legend that Suleiman had a
dream in which he was devoured by wild beasts for
failing to rebuild the walls of Jerusalem. He promptly
applied himself to this task and commemorated its
motivation by having the lions carved into its façade.

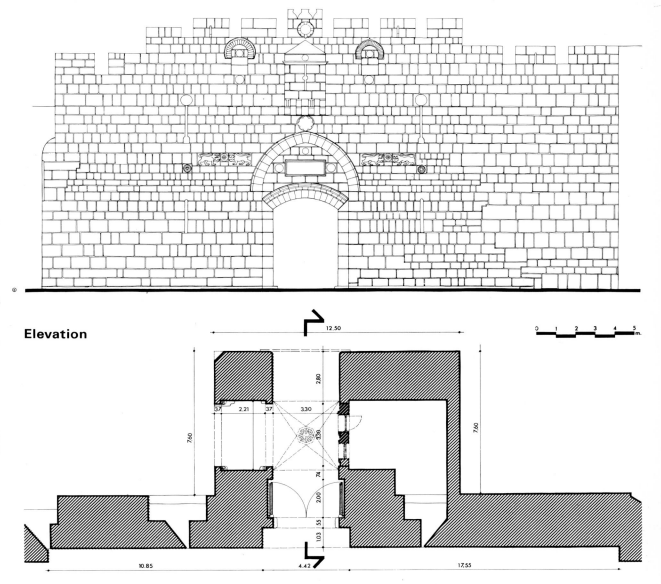

Elevation

Plan

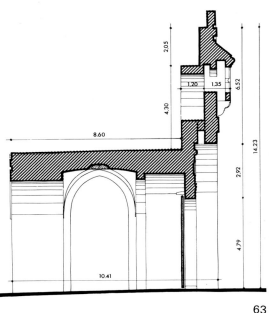

Section

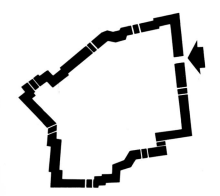

The Golden Gate

A few yards to the south of the Lions' Gate, the eastern wall of the city also becomes the east wall of the Temple Mount, and it is in this section of the wall that the Golden Gate was built. Thus in ancient days, when it was open, this gate gave direct entry to the Temple Compound. It is a large and magnificent double-arched structure which was probably originally built in the seventh century AD, and it still retains its Byzantine form though certain repairs and additions were made by Suleiman's architects. The inside of the building is divided into two rectangular chambers by a row of formidable columns which support a complicated system of decorated domes. The outer façade, which faces Gethsemane, is adorned with bold stone carvings. At its foot is a Moslem cemetery. Some of the stones used in the construction of this gate are Herodian.

The Golden Gate figures in the legends of all three religions. An early Jewish tradition holds that it is through this gate that the Messiah will enter Jerusalem. The Jews also call this gate the Gate of Mercy.

According to Christian tradition, Jesus made his last entry into Jerusalem through the Golden Gate, and the crusaders commemorated the event by inaugurating a pilgrims' procession on Palm Sunday, the only day in the year when the gate was opened. (The processional custom continues to this day, but the worshippers now enter through the Lions' Gate.)

The Moslems call it the Gate of Mercy and believe it to be the gate referred to in the Koran through which the just will pass on the Day of Judgement, 'the inner side whereof containeth mercy, while the outer side thereof is towards its doom'. The Golden Gate was finally sealed from the outside; it may still be entered from the Temple Compound.

Elevation

0 1 2 3 4 5 m.

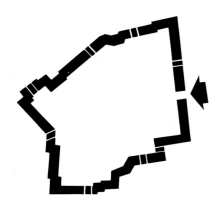

Section

Plan

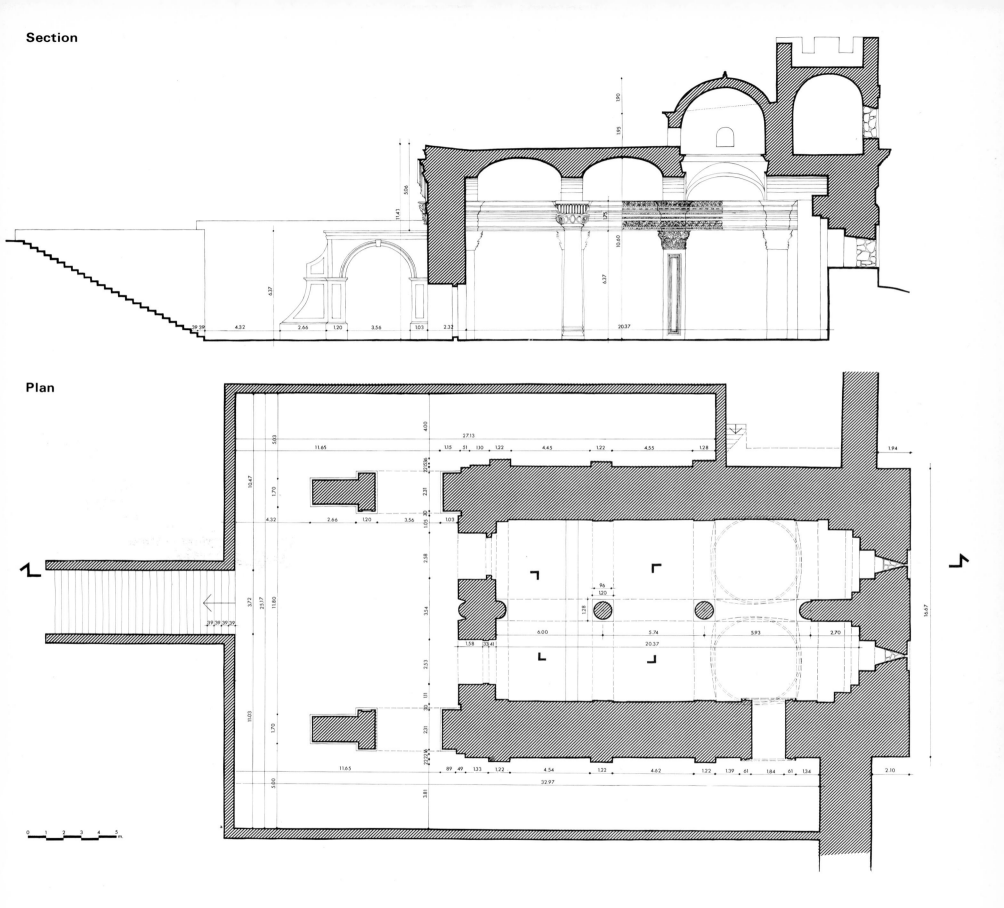

The Sealed Gates

The southern wall zigzags in a series of sharp-angled turns from the Kidron Valley in the east to the Hinnom Valley in the south and west. Its eastern section is also part of the south wall of the Temple Compound built by Herod, and it is in this section that three sealed gates are located. Two of these are Herodian, and in ancient days, when a sizeable number of Jerusalem's inhabitants lived in the area south of the Temple, these gates were the main entranceways used by the populace. They are referred to in the Talmud as the 'Gates of Hulda'.

The easternmost gate is a single-arched portal; the centre one is a triple gate; and the westernmost one is a double gate. They are of no special architectural interest, being simply openings in the wall. But they are of considerable historic interest. The Single and Triple Gates — they derive their name from the number of their portals — lead into the vast subterranean chamber, 400 square metres in area and supported by eighty-eight huge pillars which were used as hitching posts for the horses of the crusader Knights Templar. The Templars established their headquarters above it, on the southern section of the Temple Compound, the traditional site of Solomon's palace, and they therefore called the underground chamber 'King Solomon's Stables'. The structure, however, is Herodian, built to support the Temple platform.

The Double Gate, in Herod's time and up to the destruction of Jerusalem, led into an underground passage which gave onto the Temple esplanade. A flight of steps now leads down from the Mosque of El-Aksa to the interior of the Double Gate, in which there is a hall with a huge monolithic column. Its dimensions approximate the detailed description in Josephus' *Antiquities,* confirming that this gate was in use in the latter part of the Second Temple period. Only the eastern part of the Double Gate is visible from outside the city, for it is at the centre of this gate that the city wall leaves the wall of the Temple Compound in a right-angled turn to the south. It then turns westwards and after a short distance it is pierced by the Dung Gate.

1

1 The Triple Gate
2 The Single Gate
3 The Double Gate

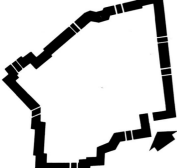

2

3

The single, double and triple entranceways to the Temple Compound. The double and triple gates were known as the gates of 'Hulda' and were the principal points of entrance for the populace at the end of the Second Temple period. The gates were sealed during the Moslem period

Zion Gate

The last of the eleven Old City Gates, described here in clockwise order from west to south, is Zion Gate, the second of the two open gates in the southern wall, located near its south-western corner just opposite Mount Zion. This gate, too, is in the form of a tower projecting from the city wall, and its façade, parallel to the wall, holds the central arched portal with a somewhat smaller archway recessed about two feet behind it, which gives onto a staggered, L-shaped passageway leading into the city. The façade, crowned by battlements in the centre of which is a fine Corinthian capital, was decorated by Suleiman's sculptors with traditional Ottoman ornamentation, half-capitals and stonecarved bosses of varied design. Embrasures on either side of the portal are framed by miniature arches which offer a play of light and shade and enrich the texture of the surrounding stone. Ancient stone stairwells lead up from the passage-chamber to a series of rooms on the upper level of the gate, probably guard-rooms, and to the observation roof, which commands a superb view both of the Old City and the history-laden countryside.

Many of Suleiman's decorations were destroyed in the 1948 War of Independence, and Zion Gate is today a battle-scarred tower, bullet-ridden and shell-pocked, a grim reminder of the bitter fighting for Jerusalem which marked the birth of the State of Israel.

This gate is closest to Mount Zion and bears the scars of the battles fought in the 1948 War of Independence

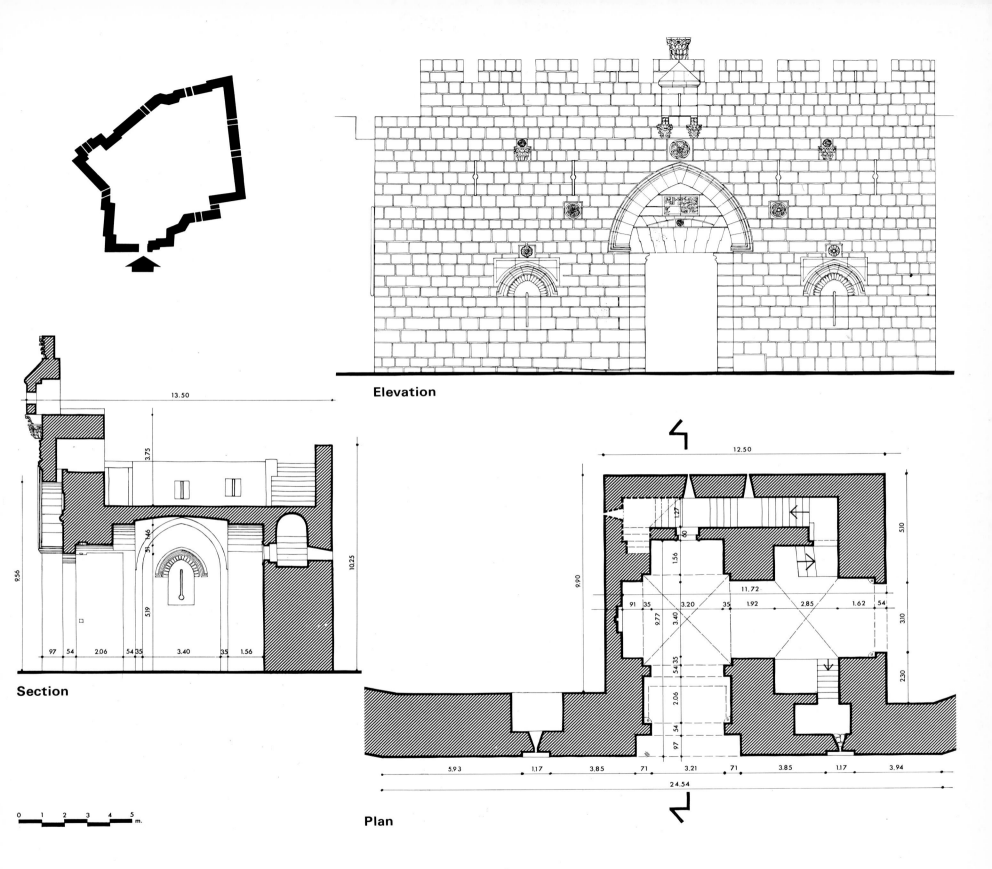

Elevation

Section

13.50

3.75

9.56

10.25

5.19

31.46

97 | 54 | 2.06 | 54 35 | 3.40 | 35 | 1.56

0 1 2 3 4 5 m.

Plan

12.50

9.90

5.10

3.10

2.30

11.72

1.27

.60

1.56

91 | 35 | 3.20 | 35 | 1.92 | 2.85 | 1.62 | 54

9.77

3.40

54 35

2.06

54

97

5.93 | 1.17 | 3.85 | .71 | 3.21 | .71 | 3.85 | 1.17 | 3.94

24.54

Planning Problems and Proposals

With the reunion of Jerusalem in June 1967, one of the immediate townplanning aims was the restoration to their former glory of the walls and gates of the Old City. The most critical sections are in the north wall between Damascus Gate and the New Gate and the west wall between Zahal Square, at the north-west corner, and Jaffa Gate. It is along these two stretches that the densely built-up areas, mostly commercial quarters, of new Jerusalem adjoin the Old City walls without a break in the terrain, and all that separates them are narrow, unsightly, overcrowded streets and pavements. Piles of rubble and debris were banked against the wall, and the strip near Jaffa Gate was covered with provisional buildings and improvised shacks erected under the Ottomans in the last century, effectively blocking the view of the gate. The 1929 Townplanning Scheme of the Mandatory Government recommended the clearance of these ugly constructions, but the good intentions remained unfulfilled, and the slum area remained — and spread.

Only after the Six Day War were the rubble, shacks and derelict buildings removed and the western city wall and Jaffa Gate restored to view. However, very much more needed to be done, and a new project is now under execution (see page 194) for the comprehensive development of this area, an ill-defined space which thousands of motorists and pedestrians pass each day. There was only a narrow strip of pavement for pedestrians, and so they tended to crowd into the road, seeking to gain an approach view of wall, Citadel and the Jaffa Gate without being run over by a car. The motorist, in turn, was busy negotiating both traffic and jay-walkers — and looking for a place to park. The projected plan includes the proposal to turn Zahal Square (close to the New Gate) into a paved garden-plaza and to build a pedestrian route from there to the Jaffa Gate.

The same architectural approach has been adopted in the site-improvement proposals for the Damascus Gate. The moat below it has been partially excavated and the levels of successive historical periods are now exposed to view, the lowest being the stratum of huge stones from the Herodian period. It is thus possible to gain from this gate, in a measure unmatched by any other, a visual comprehension of the organic growth of the Old City through the ages. The present plan calls for the excavation of the entire moat so as to bring to light more of the magnificent Herodian masonry and to link the moat by a series of staircases and ramps with the already excavated forecourt of the Herodian gate and up to the interior plaza of the present Damascus Gate. This redesigned and rebuilt area, with its varying levels of the different periods, will dramatise the historical development of the city. The small garden strip along the north wall is already being extended, replanted and repaved as far as the New Gate. It will be continued up to the Zahal Square plaza and thus connect with the promenade up to Jaffa Gate and terminate at the small and charming garden plaza recently laid just outside the Citadel.

The southern and eastern walls and the part of the western city wall south of Jaffa Gate are skirted by much steeper slopes, and they are to form an integral part of the Jerusalem National Park, a green garden belt fringing the city walls through the Kidron and Hinnom valleys. But the main challenge and task for the city fathers, architects and planners is to fashion a spatial connection, functionally well-defined and architecturally well-designed, between the two most important entrances to the Old City — Jaffa Gate and Damascus Gate — to serve the growing population of new Jerusalem. Fortunately there are free and empty areas in front of both gates.

A considerable stretch of undeveloped land fronting Damascus Gate is ideally located to provide an organic link between the existing Arab commercial centre and the walled town. A similar undeveloped area exists near the Jaffa Gate which can form a public and commercial link between the Old City and the present overcrowded Jewish commercial centre opposite the gate. The plan envisages underground garages for 750—1,000 cars on both sites. The areas above these car-parks may be developed as large public plazas, with appropriate civic buildings, where sizeable crowds can gather for cultural and ceremonial events.

It will be seen that in replanning these areas priority has been given to pedestrians, as the area immediately adjoining the gates is reserved for their use only. Motor traffic, both public and private, will terminate at the underground car-parks, and the entry of vehicles into the Old City will be restricted to the hours of the early morning and late evening, and even then only for service and emergency needs. The Old City is to remain a town without wheels, a town of pedestrians, as it was in past generations.

Chapter 5   Structure and Architecture of the Old City

Structure and Architecture of the Old City

In its structural layout, the Old City forms an organic townplanning entity. It is a living city, well-based economically and socially. It is not simply a monument to its glorious past, nor is it an archaeological relic to be preserved like a museum piece for its historic and architectural value alone. Throughout the centuries, to this very day, it has been both a vibrant spiritual and cultural centre, with established religious institutions of high status, and also a flourishing centre of trade and handicrafts. Its religious life in particular springs from age-old traditions, and Jerusalem is held dear by millions of people, some of whom are moved to spend their lives in the Holy City, many more to visit it as pilgrim or tourist, and countless numbers at least to harbour the hope of seeing it before they die.

But even in purely physical terms, Jerusalem has much to offer. It enjoys a most equable climate, with a dry heat in summer (unlike the sultry and humid coastal plain), always blessed by cool nights, and long periods of brilliant sunshine in winter. (There are an average of three hundred sunny days a year.) Its refreshing mountain air is as yet unspoiled by pollution. It commands a unique and varied micro-landscape around three of the city walls, while the townscape within is equally unique, marked by vaulted alleyways, narrow lanes open to the sky, forecourts and interior plazas, stone-paved and bordered by trees.

The Old City, to be sure, also has the deficiencies which are all too common in old towns whose population has grown and faces the needs of the twentieth century. There is an inadequate infrastructure, an absence of certain vital public services, and streets and buildings which have deteriorated, notably in the overcrowded Moslem Quarter, and which call desperately for comprehensive restoration. However, the provision of missing services and the problem of reconstruction, repair and new building may be remedied without much difficulty, and indeed much has been done in the last three years by the Municipality. Certain essential improvements have

already been carried out, and several comprehensive plans for future development are in the process of completion and are to be implemented without delay.

Today's Old City has a population of 24,000. More than half are densely concentrated in the Moslem Quarter, living in overcrowded slums. Some of its residents should be moved to new housing quarters in the special zone proposed in our scheme and the vacated slums renovated. (Several houses have already been built for this purpose in this zone.) The Jewish Quarter, completely destroyed during the 1948 War of Independence and during the period of Jordanian rule, is in the process of being rebuilt and rehabilitated.

From reports of field surveys and other data we assembled, we reached the conclusion that the number of residents in the Old City should not exceed 20,000. In reaching this figure, we have taken into account the proposed slum clearance programme for the Moslem Quarter and the new housing schemes for the Jewish Quarter. We have also taken into consideration the numerous public buildings which already exist, particularly in the Christian and Armenian Quarters, such as monasteries, schools, youth clubs, clinics, to serve the social educational, cultural and religious life of the communities, and the projected new schools, clubs and kindergartens in the Moslem Quarter and the new public and residential buildings under construction in the Jewish Quarter.

Of special interest is the fact, which emerged from our study of Jerusalem's development throughout history, that up to the middle of the nineteenth century the built-up quarters inside the Old City did not extend right up to the walls but were separated from them by a belt of open space, covered by gardens and reserved for the public. Only later did the buildings, mostly those of ecclesiastical institutions, creep up to the walls and devour much of the open public space. Many of them, moreover, were allowed to rise to inordinate heights, towering above the

walls in unharmonious incongruity, as can so readily, and regretfully, be seen today both from inside and outside the walls. In the outline scheme for the Old City, we propose that a final stop be put to this unaesthetic development and that the unbuilt spaces just inside the wall should be extended and remain public open spaces free of any buildings.

The size of the Old City, together with its narrow lanes and alleys, is characteristic of — and just right for — a pedestrian town, serviced only by mule and donkey traffic. There are, however, a few one-way streets for motor vehicles, and these will be retained under the scheme, although, as we have indicated earlier, these will be restricted to service and emergency transport and only at specified hours during the day.

The Old City is divided into four clearly defined quarters, each differing from the others in architecture and community origin. The four are the Armenian, Christian, Moslem and Jewish quarters.

Architecture

The homogeneous townscape of the residential streets and quarters is dominated by an impressive variety of domes, towers and minarets, which can be seen from everywhere, both inside and outside the city walls. The unexpected vistas up or down the narrow streets are usually terminated by a Christian tower, a Jewish dome or a Moslem minaret. The roofscape of the Old City's quarters, seen from a higher building or from the hills outside the walls, is even more impressive and striking. Domes and arches, Byzantine, Romanesque or Ottoman, vary in size and shape and are interspersed with church towers and minarets, many of them from the Mameluke period. They create a mosaic pattern rich in form and colour.

There are several buildings in the Old City of Jerusalem which are of outstanding architectural grace and value. The most striking complex, which constitutes the city's spectacular landmark, is the Dome of the Rock and the even more magnificent and ancient platform of the Temple Mount, spacious and beautiful, upon which the Dome stands. The Dome of the Rock is an octagonal structure, consisting of a wooden dome, over 20 metres in diameter, which rests on four piers and twelve columns placed in a circle, three slender columns alternating with each pier. Around this inner circle of columns runs an intermediate octagonal arcade, consisting of arches again supported by eight piers and sixteen columns. The outer walls form a large octagon whose eight sides are over 20 metres high, each pierced by seven windows. The decoration is rich and splendid; the exterior is partly covered by marble panelling and glass mosaics on a shiny gilded background; the internal arcades and walls are covered with mosaics and marble panelling. Architecturally, the Dome of the Rock represents a clear, geometric and organic form of a spacious octagon, crowned by a gilded dome; the details and decorative additions have great charm and reflect a natural architectural continuity through the successive historical periods.

The Dome dominates the huge Herodian Temple platform, on which, through the centuries, small minarets, towers and fountains were erected, clusters of trees planted and broad flights of steps added. The total result is a piazza of magnificence, peaceful and harmonious, spacious but in the correct human scale, its four sides bordered — with charming naiveté — by slender arches. There are clear and simple space relationships between platform, dome, arches, steps, minarets and the small sculptured structures studding the compound. According to Jewish and Moslem tradition, the Temple Mount and its rock are believed to be the centre of the world. Here was the scene of the sacrifice of Isaac; here stood the altar of the first Jewish Temple; and from this rock, Mohammed, in a dream, is said to have ascended to heaven, after reaching Jerusalem from Mecca in a single night on the back of 'Al Burak', his magic steed.

Another landmark is the Church of the Holy Sepulchre, centrepiece of the Christian Quarter. It is an architectural conglomerate: the rectangular shape of Constantine's edifice was changed by the crusaders into the form of a cross in the Romanesque style, and the four shrines were united under a single roof, the rotunda of the sepulchre dome following Constantine's design and rising on its original foundations. Further chapels and cloisters, of diverse forms, were added throughout the centuries. Its mixed architectural character is the product of frequent repair and restoration since its original creation in the fourth century AD. The Church of the Holy Sepulchre is a sanctuary shared by the major Christian denominations, and at festival time it offers a variety of ritual ceremonies under the same roof.

The two outstanding buildings which dominated the Jewish Quarter were synagogues. One, the Hurva, had a clear space conception of a big quadrangle crowned by a large dome with four strong corner pillars. It was completely destroyed by the Jordanians, and plans for a new synagogue to be built on the site are currently being prepared by the architect Louis Kahn. The second was a group of four synagogues, chief of which was the Rabbi Yohanan ben Zakkai Synagogue, the entire structural complex an impressive cluster of domes and courtyards evoking a mood of spiritual tranquillity. Their first construction dates back to the sixteenth century, when some of the Jews exiled from Spain began to settle in Jerusalem. They were destroyed and rebuilt time and again and thus 'grew', rather than were built, over a period of four hundred years. The buildings were partially destroyed during the War of Independence and their current reconstruction, which began immediately after the Six Day War, is almost complete (see project on page 184).

However, it is not these few individual buildings which give the Old City its special character and unique atmosphere. These are created by the total townscape: the winding lanes uphill and downhill; the alleys and stone stairways darting off them and suddenly widening into miniature plazas or terminating in an unexpected garden or court; the noise and bustle in one quarter, the gentle peace in another; the odd juxtaposition of monumental building with narrow bazaar, or of a medieval passage with an architectural gem, like the exquisitely proportioned biblical Pool of Hezekiah (alas deteriorated through neglect; see project, page 172). Above all, there are the varied layers of antiquity, eloquent chapters in the dramatic autobiography of an age-old city that is still very much alive.

The crowning features of Jerusalem's townscape are its plazas. At one end of the scale are the handsome ones of modest size at the outlets of the two main city gates, Damascus Gate and Jaffa Gate. They are well proportioned in form and space, though there is some spoilage by modernistic building, and they are lined by shops and restaurants. Only modest architectural changes at little cost are required to renovate them (see project on page 169). At the other end of the scale are the two vast plazas in the Temple area. With the clearance of slums and the debris of destruction in the eastern part of the Jewish Quarter, there is now a huge, paved platform open to the sky in front of the Western Wall, large enough for gatherings of tens of thousands at Jewish festivals and fast days. Work continues on the architectural design of this plaza, which will be finalised upon completion of the adjacent archaeological excavations. The second piazza is the Temple Mount itself, which we have already described, the high and formidable platform set amid the historic valleys and hills of Judea, which has contributed so much, and for so long, to the beauty of Jerusalem.

*The quiet streets, alleys and courts of the
Armenian compound
left The arched entrance to the main street*

1

2

1 Low passageway leading to the public and private squares of the Armenian compound
2 Detail of external staircase on the main square
3 Side entrance to St James Church. Note the elaborate ironwork of the door

3

1

The Christian Quarter

The Christian Quarter is in the north-west, the highest part of the Old City. It covers an area of 45 acres and has 4,300 inhabitants. It abounds with ecclesiastical structures representing almost every Christian denomination and sect, but the most sacred and ancient in origin is the Church of the Holy Sepulchre, stemming from Byzantine and crusader times. The various religious institutions provide extensive community services, including elementary and secondary schools and youth clubs. The quarter, its streets, houses and public buildings are clean and well cared for, and all its structures are of local stone.

To the south of the Holy Sepulchre is the Muristan (from the old Arabic name for 'hospital'), the site of the crusader Hospital of St John, cradle of the Knights of St John, who are also known as the Hospitalers. The present Muristan, preserving the old name, was built in 1905 as a centre for the wholesale textile and clothing trade and a workshop area mostly for cobblers and goldsmiths. To its immediate north and south are the souvenir and art shops which cater to the pilgrims and tourists who flock to the Christian sites. The Muristan, with its sloping tiled roofs, stands out from the other buildings in the Old City, which favour flat roofs and stone cupolas. Since the business conducted in the Muristan is largely wholesale, and the roads which skirt it are fairly wide, this is a relatively quiet area, and it seems even more quiet after the contrasting bustle of the adjacent bazaars.

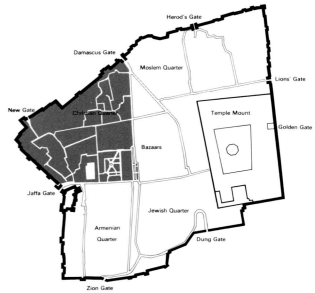

1 The domes and towers of Jerusalem's churches
2 Side entrance to the Church of the Holy Sepulchre

1

2

3

1   The courtyard of the Umariya Boys'
    School on the original site of the
    Herodian fortress of Antonia. This is the
    First Station of the Cross
2   Detail of a wall
3   The bell-tower of the church of St John
    the Baptist
4   Via Dolorosa (which runs partly in the
    Moslem and partly in the Christian
    Quarters)
5–7   Street scenes

4

5

6

7

Originally all the courtyards, piazzas and streets of the Old City were paved with stones. In the wealthier, more established quarters, the stone pavements have been preserved, while in the poorer quarters they have been neglected and partly replaced by less attractive and durable materials, like asphalt. It is the intention of the planners to restore all the neglected pavements to their original stone pattern

1 Many of the streets in the hilly Old City
  are stepped and arched
2 Detail of Mameluke building in the Moslem
  Quarter
3 Vaulted Mameluke gateway to the Harem
  esh-Sharif

3

One of the four splendid arched entrances
to the Dome of the Rock
opposite *Details of religious structures of
various Moslem periods*

The Jewish Quarter

The Jewish Quarter is located in the south-east, standing, like the adjacent Armenian Quarter, within the area of the Upper City of the Second Temple period. It covers 35 acres and in May 1948 its population numbered 5,300. While there was a good deal of petty commerce and handicrafts, life in this quarter centred almost wholly round its numerous synagogues and rabbinical seminaries. Many of these were destroyed in the 1948 War of Independence, and some of the outstanding religious buildings which survived the battles were deliberately razed by the Jordanians during their subsequent nineteen-year occupation. In all those years, no Jew was allowed to set foot there. With its liberation in June 1967 and the reunification of Jerusalem, a special body was established to plan and implement the reconstruction and development of the Jewish Quarter. Many of the building projects in its programme for the reconstruction of destroyed dwellings, streets, synagogues and seminaries are nearing completion; and several of the damaged synagogues and other structures have already been restored (see project on page 176).

Concurrent with the preparatory work of clearing the rubble and digging for the foundations of the new buildings, Professor Nahman Avigad of the Hebrew University carried out archaeological excavations in the quarter. Among his important discoveries are relics belonging to the seventh century BC, the period of the Judean kings; ruins of Hasmonean structures dating back to the second and first centuries BC; remains of the Herodian period from the end of the first century BC; and the grim evidence of destruction of Jewish dwellings by Titus in AD 70. One of the Jewish structures he uncovered was in exactly the same state as it had been left when destroyed by fire 1,900 years ago. The debris, which contained numerous fire-proof artefacts — including coins (which confirmed the date of the destruction) — had never been cleared.

The outstanding feature of the Jewish Quarter is, and has been since the destruction of the Second Temple in AD 70, the Western Wall. It is the most sacred Jewish site, the Holy Place to which Jews journeying from distant lands throughout the centuries have come to pray. The area fronting the Wall was in a sad state of deterioration, covered by dilapidated buildings, some in a state of near collapse. This area was cleared and a huge stone-paved plaza laid down soon after the Six Day War, so that it was able to serve the tens of thousands of worshippers who were now able to flock to the site on Sabbaths and Jewish festivals. It also serves as a ceremonial plaza for national and religious celebrations. The archaeological excavations of Professor Binyamin Mazar are proceeding immediately to the south and south-west of the Wall and he too has made discoveries of the utmost importance, including the remains — some of them very well preserved — of structures ranging from the seventh century BC. Particularly impressive are the Herodian ruins. The Western Wall plaza will be given its final shape when these archaeological excavations are completed.

An 18th-century lithograph of the Jewish Quarter
left *Decorative interior of the Dome of the Rock*

2

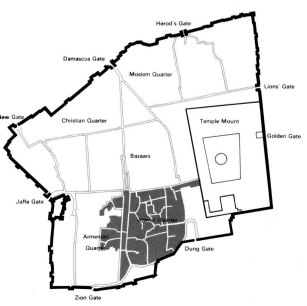

1

Chapter 6   The Old City Survey and Outline Scheme

The Old City Survey and Outline Scheme

Topography

The walls of the Old City enclose two parallel and undulating ridges running north to south. The central valley dividing them, called the Tyropoeon Valley in the first century, has largely been filled by the debris of centuries, so that the Old City today appears to be a plateau. The Temple Mount lies on the northern part of the eastern ridge and is 740 metres above sea level. The Christian Quarter stands on the northern part of the western ridge and is the highest location in the city, at 785 metres. On the southern part of the western ridge stands the Armenian Quarter, and rising to its immediate south is Mount Zion, 770 metres high. In the Second Temple period, Mount Zion lay within the city walls. It was excluded from Aelia Capitolina, enclosed once again in the fifth century, and again excluded in the sixteenth century during Suleiman's reconstruction, so that today it still lies just outside the walls. The Jewish Quarter in the southeast corner is, at 730 metres, the lowest part of the city.

Ancient Water Systems

With only modest water resources, Jerusalem, since early times, has had to improvise systems for water conservation. Apart from a few elaborate schemes, the most common system throughout the centuries was the collection of rainwater in natural cisterns along the *wadis* and its transfer by conduit to artificial reservoirs.

The major source of Jerusalem's water since time immemorial was the Gihon Spring, in the Kidron Valley, and a number of wells. The most elaborate and the most ancient water conservation system was that undertaken by the Judean king Hezekiah at the end of the eighth century BC. He sealed the outside of the Gihon cave, to deny access to an invader, and then cut a 600-yard tunnel which led the water by gravity flow under the south-eastern part of the city as it existed in his day (south of the Temple Mount) and out to a reservoir or pool inside the city at a point where the ground is lower. This was the Siloam pool. The purpose was to ensure access to water in time of siege. The event is recorded in the Bible, and the tunnel, discovered in 1880, may be seen today. (A tablet with an inscription in classical Hebrew describing how the tunnel was dug was found at the same time, and is known as the Siloam Inscription.)

Two other important water systems were carried out in the first century BC. These were the construction of two aqueducts which brought water to Jerusalem from Solomon's Pools near Bethlehem and from the nearby hills. There is scholarly controversy as to who built them, but it is generally considered that one was constructed by the Hasmoneans and the other by Herod and that the earlier one was later repaired in the first century AD by Pontius Pilate.

There are several ancient cisterns which are of interest. One is the pool in the basement of the Ecce Homo Convent, which is still filled with water. Indeed, during the Jordanian occupation, with an inadequate water supply, this water was used for all purposes except drinking. Another cistern is the Israel Pool, just north-west of the Temple Compound, which was in use throughout the Ottoman period. It was closed by the Mandatory Administration because it was a breeding ground for mosquitos. Captain Charles Warren made a survey in the last century with proposals for its restoration. The celebrated Pool of Bethzetha, mentioned in the New Testament, lies within the precincts of the crusader Church of St Anne. There have been archaeological excavations on this site, and remains were found of the first church to be constructed here — on part of the pool — during Byzantine times.

Today, the Old City — like the new Jerusalem — is well supplied with water, for after the Six Day War it was incorporated into the national water network of Israel.

Aerial view of the Old City

The map contains the following labels:

- El-Hagg Pool
- Pool of Bethesda
- Legerii Pool
- Myriam's Pool
- Strution Pool
- Pool of Israel
- Twin Pools
- The water channel connecting the Mammilla Pool with the Hezekiah Pool
- Hezekiah's Pool
- The Upper Pool
- Course of waterbed before the building of the Temple platform
- Aqueduct
- The Jebusite Sinnor
- Gihon Spring
- Hezekiah's Tunnel
- Sultan's Pool

Source: M. Hecker, 'Jerusalem's Water Supply in Ancient Times', in M. Avi-Yonah, ed., *Jerusalem*, 1956.

Ancient Water Systems

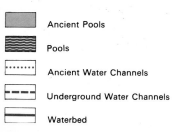

- ▨ Ancient Pools
- ▨ Pools
- ⋯ Ancient Water Channels
- ‒ ‒ Underground Water Channels
- ── Waterbed

The Bedrock Structure of the Old City

The Old City is bounded in the east by the steep Kidron Valley and in the west and south by the curving Valley of Hinnom. Only in the north and north-west is there level terrain, and this topographical feature explains why the new town has developed in these directions.

The Christian Quarter stands on the bedrock. The Jewish and Moslem quarters are built upon the accumulated ruins of structures belonging to more ancient settlement periods. Indeed, as we have seen in chapter II, recent archaeological excavations in the Jewish Quarter revealed that the first Israelite houses built in this part of the city date as far back as the seventh century BC.

We see from sections D-D and E-E that in the north, the ground inside the Old City is on the same broad level as the ground outside. However, Suleiman Road, which skirts the north wall, is lower. This is because this road, with its celebrated grottos of Jeremiah and Zedekiah, lies along the base of a huge stone quarry.

Key-map of Sections Appearing on the Opposite Page

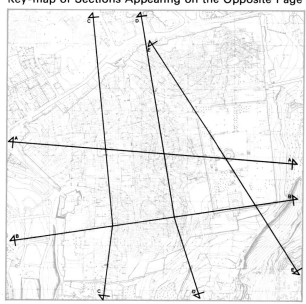

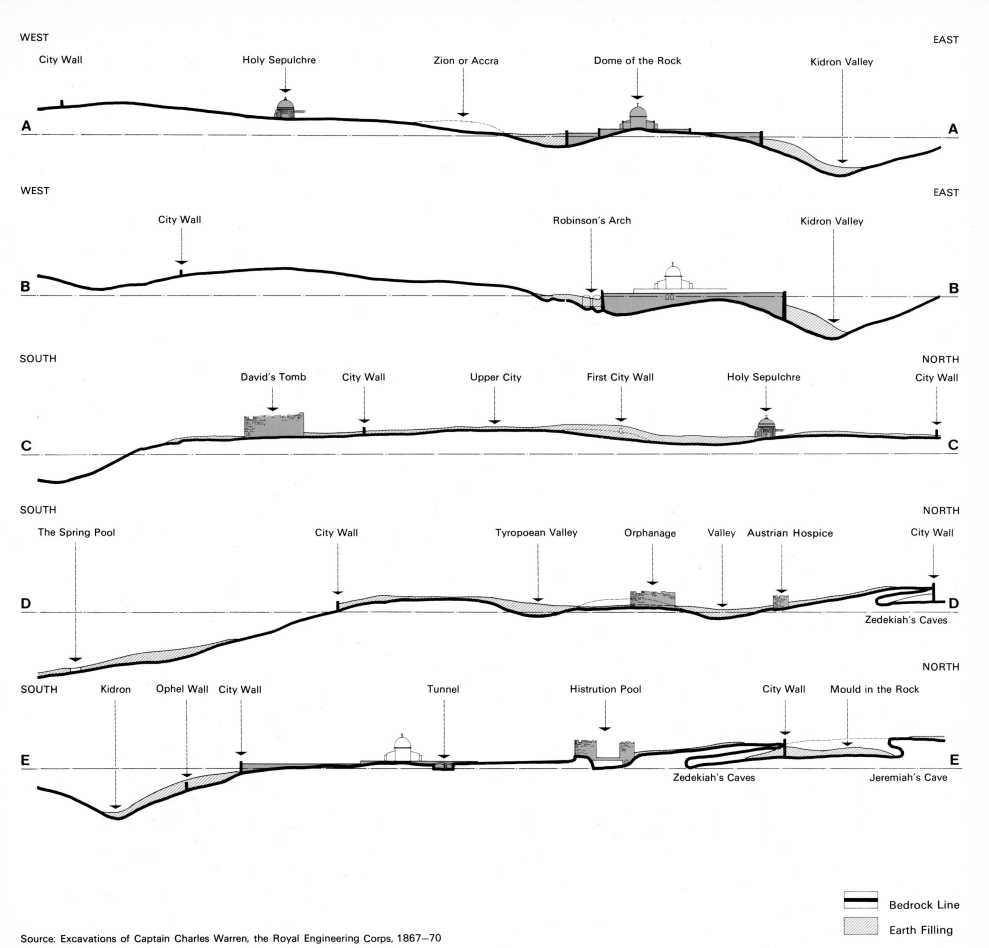

WEST   EAST

City Wall   Holy Sepulchre   Zion or Accra   Dome of the Rock   Kidron Valley

A   A

WEST   EAST

City Wall   Robinson's Arch   Kidron Valley

B   B

SOUTH   NORTH

David's Tomb   City Wall   Upper City   First City Wall   Holy Sepulchre   City Wall

C   C

SOUTH   NORTH

The Spring Pool   City Wall   Tyropoean Valley   Orphanage   Valley   Austrian Hospice   City Wall

D   D

Zedekiah's Caves

NORTH

SOUTH   Kidron   Ophel Wall   City Wall   Tunnel   Histrution Pool   City Wall   Mould in the Rock

E   E

Zedekiah's Caves   Jeremiah's Cave

Bedrock Line

Earth Filling

Source: Excavations of Captain Charles Warren, the Royal Engineering Corps, 1867–70

113

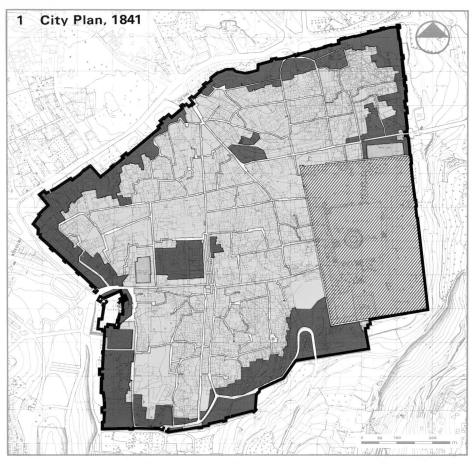

1 City Plan, 1841

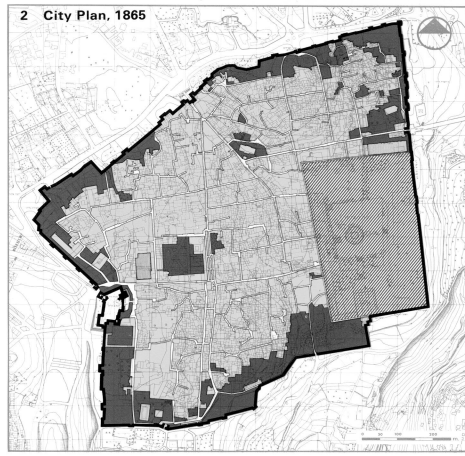

2 City Plan, 1865

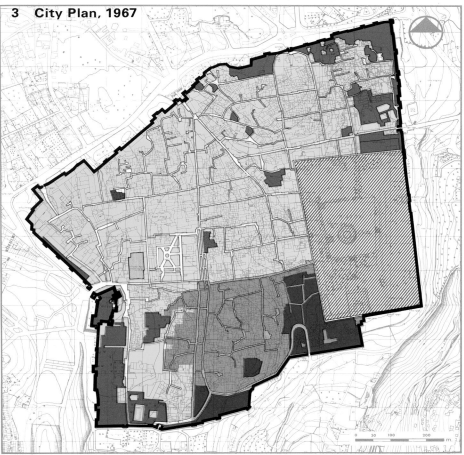

3 City Plan, 1967

Open Spaces

The first accurate map of the Old City was that drawn in 1841 by Lts Symonds and Aldrich of the British Army, and it shows that just inside the city walls there was a broad green belt free of buildings. By the 1860s, the amount of open space in the Old City had deteriorated somewhat, as can be seen from the 1863 map by the French Captain Gelis and the map of the British explorer C. W. Wilson. They show that near the Damascus Gate, building was already starting to creep up to the wall.

By the end of the nineteenth century, with improved political relations between the Ottoman Empire and several European states, the Christian denominations extended their building activities. Several new churches and other structures were erected close to the walls (indeed, some were built right up against the walls), a number of them higher than, and towering over, the adjacent ramparts. This is particularly true in the Christian Quarter (St Saviour's Convent and Church and the Latin Patriarchate near the New Gate), but it also occurred in the Jewish Quarter, with the construction of the *batei machase* (alms houses) only a few yards from the wall. In the Moslem Quarter, there was serious encroachment on the open space inside the walls by the building of numerous houses. All these structures considerably reduced the green belt running along the inside of the walls and obscured their architectural grandeur. It is strongly recommended that the open space and the green belt inside the walls be preserved and, where possible, extended. The inside of the walls should be kept free of any buildings.

⌐_⌐	The City Wall
░	Built-up Area
▓	Open Space
▒	Pool

Vehicular and Pedestrian Circulation

With the expansion of the city beyond the walls that began a hundred years ago and has rapidly accelerated in the last seventy years, the Old City has been brought face to face with the universal conflict between man and vehicle. There are three gates through which motorised traffic can enter the city: the New Gate, which was opened in 1887 and whence an asphalt road leads into the Christian Quarter; Jaffa Gate, into which a breach was made in 1898 to allow the German Kaiser Wilhelm II to enter the city in state and from which there is a main thoroughfare for private vehicles which skirts the Armenian Quarter, hugging the inside of the city walls and exiting at the Dung Gate; and the Lions' Gate through which vehicular traffic can enter as far as El-Wad Street.

It is an urgent concern of the planners that the Old City be kept free of motorised traffic, as far as possible, and that its character as a pedestrian town be preserved. Motorised traffic should only be allowed in special service lanes, catering to the immediate needs of the population, and for emergencies, and it should be restricted to fixed hours in the early morning and late evening. The cobbled streets, which are for the most part steep and stepped, would continue to be served by donkeys and mules. (Plans are being prepared which would nevertheless provide a more convenient and efficient means of transport for essential public services.)

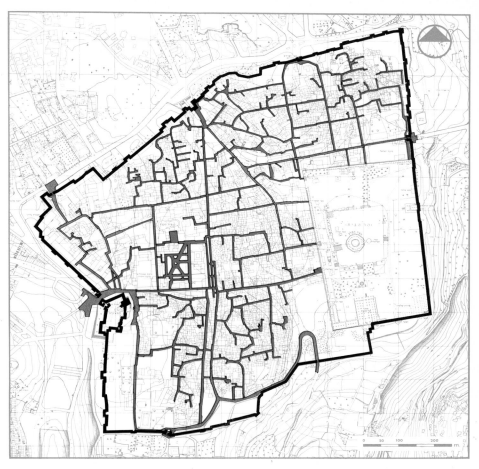

Pedestrians

Vehicles

Street Surfacing

The map at right, based on data from the Ministry of Transport and from a special field survey which the planners carried out early in 1969, shows the existing pattern of pedestrian streets and lanes as compared with the network of motor-roads. The Outline Town-planning Scheme proposes only one motor-road — the thoroughfare from the Jaffa Gate to the Dung Gate (see page 123).

The streets and alleyways of the Old City were originally paved in stone. As this paving deteriorated, it was resurfaced in concrete or asphalt. This was particularly true of roads used by motor traffic. It is strongly recommended that all new surfacing inside the Old City should follow the original stone-paving pattern.

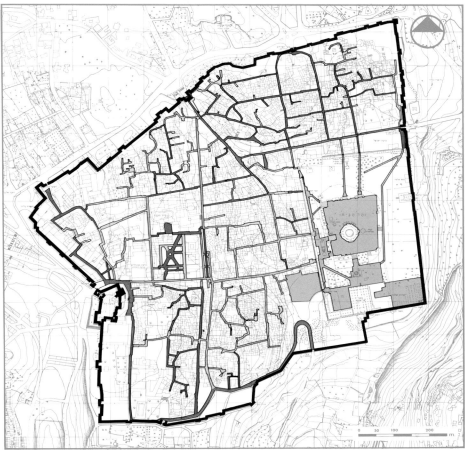

Asphalt

Concrete

Stone-paving

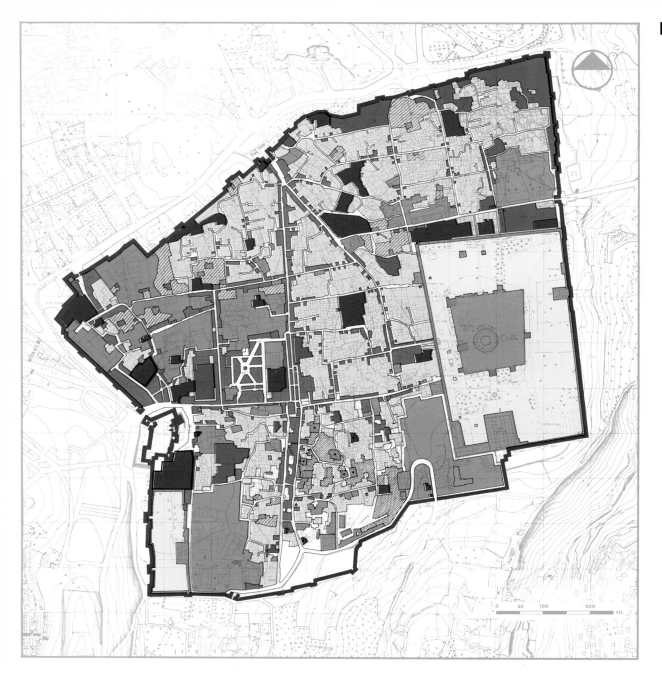

Religious Institutions

Housing within Religious Compounds

Residential Area

Community Services

Commerce and Workshops

Open Spaces

Ruins

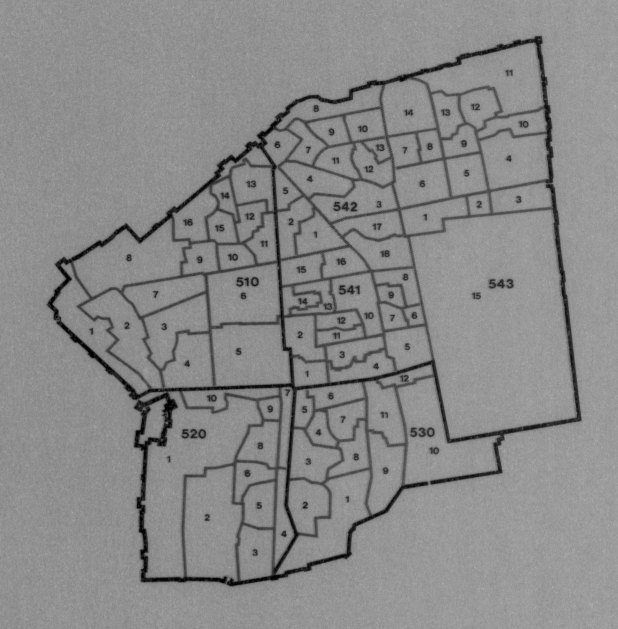

Statistical Division in the Old City

Sub-quarter

Statistical Area Boundary

Census-cell Boundary

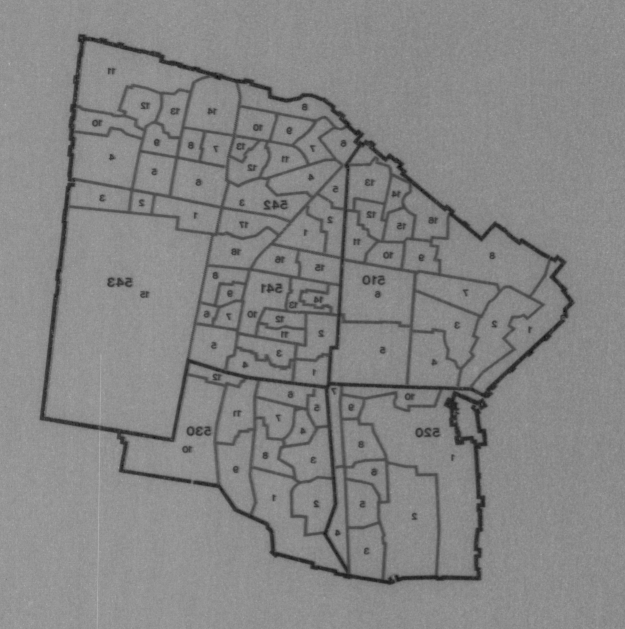

Statistical Division in the Old City

Population Density

A census of the entire population of the Old City was carried out at the end of 1967. The results are shown in the population density map. It will be seen that the areas of least density are those round the Temple Mount and the Western Wall: 0 — 4 persons per dunam. The highest density was registered in various parts — notably the centre — of the Moslem Quarter, with 140 persons per dunam (560 per acre).

The planners believe that the number of residents in the Old City should not exceed 20,000. In reaching this figure, they have taken into account the proposed slum clearance programme for the Moslem Quarter and the new housing schemes for the Jewish Quarter. They have also taken into consideration the many public buildings which already exist, particularly in the Christian and Armenian quarters, such as monasteries, schools, youth clubs and clinics, to serve the social, educational, cultural and religious life of the communities, the projected new schools, clubs and kindergartens in the Moslem Quarter and the new public and residential buildings under construction in the Jewish Quarter.

The data in this survey derives from the Tax Assessment Register of the Jerusalem Municipality and from the intensive field survey which was carried out at the beginning of 1969. Since there was no exact map of the Old City which indicated the blocks and parcellation, the planners had to devise their own to show the exact location of each building and open space and their different uses according to the tax register.

It will be seen from the map that the highest concentration of public and religious buildings is to be found in the Christian Quarter, the south-west corner of the Armenian Quarter and the area around the Temple Mount. The highest concentration of residential buildings is in the Moslem Quarter. (Also densely populated — by Moslems — during the Jordanian occupation from 1948 to 1967 was the destroyed Jewish Quarter.)

The few open spaces still remaining in the Old City are situated mostly in the north-east corner of the Moslem Quarter. These should be protected and reserved for public gardens and parks.

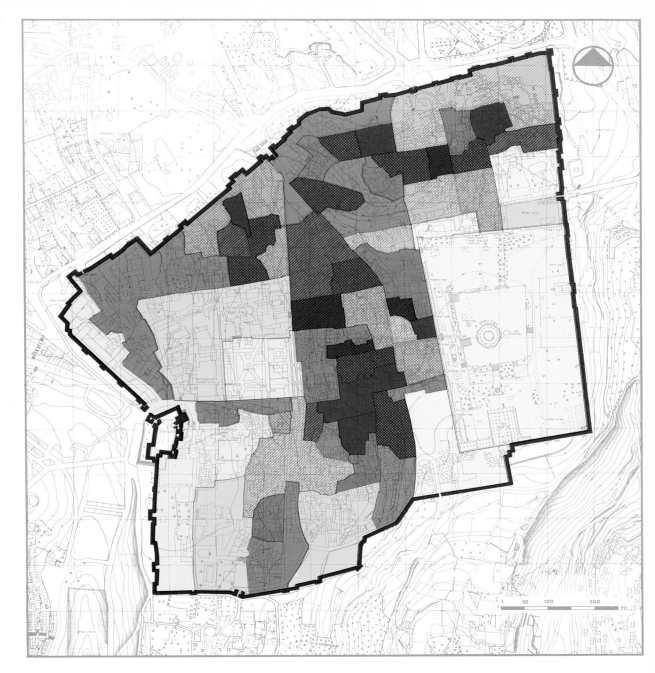

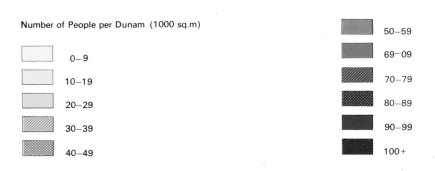

Number of People per Dunam (1000 sq.m)

0—9	50—59
10—19	69—09
20—29	70—79
30—39	80—89
40—49	90—99
	100+

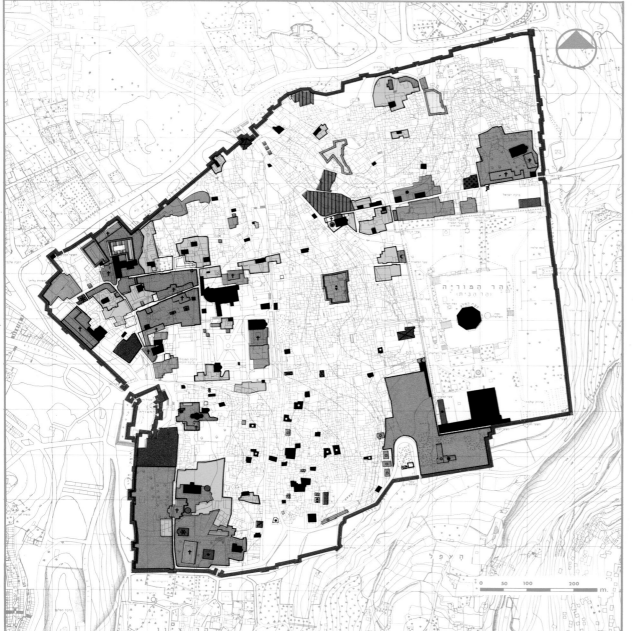

Public and Community Services

1 Community Services

	Educational and Research Institution
	School under Construction
♦	Vocational School
†	Christian Seminar
☾	Moslem Madrassah
⊙	Jewish Yeshiva
•	Research Institute

2 Public Services

	Police Station
	Municipality
•	Post Office
✕	Public Conveniences
	Electric Transformer Station

a Health Services

	Private Doctor
	Public Clinic
‖‖	Hospital
‖‖	Hospital for Chronic Diseases

b Religious Services

	Holy Place—Building
	Holy Place—Area
†	Patriarchate Administration
☾	Waqf Administration
⊙	Jewish Religious Council

c Welfare Services

	Welfare Centre
	Orphanage
	Hospice

3 Cultural Services

■	Museum
✳	Library
	Community Club
•	Synagogues (ruined)

	Community Services
	Public Services
	Religious Services
	Health Services
	Cultural Services
	Welfare Services
	Public Garden

Religious Institutions

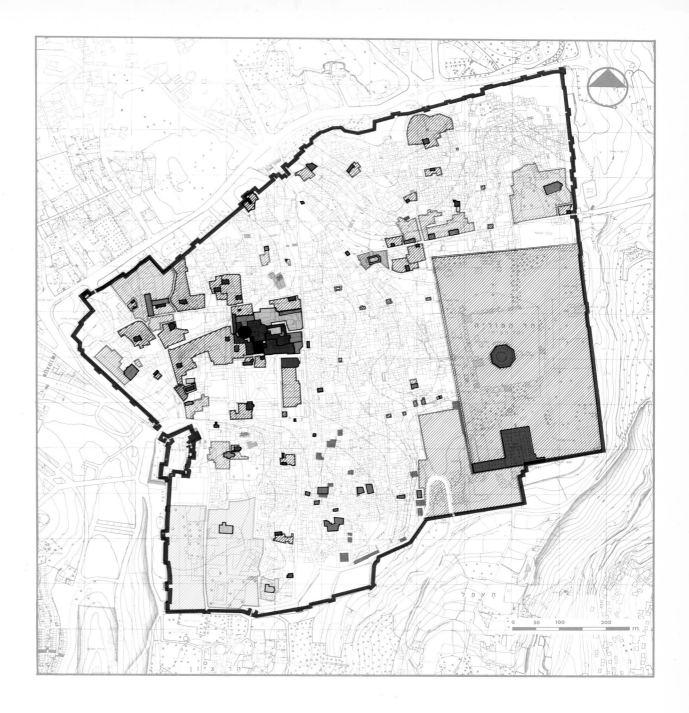

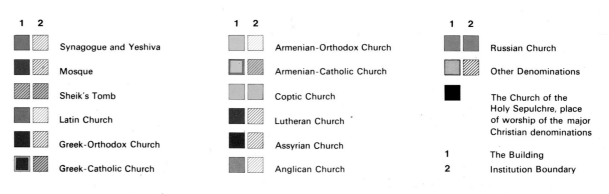

1	2	
		Synagogue and Yeshiva
		Mosque
		Sheik's Tomb
		Latin Church
		Greek-Orthodox Church
		Greek-Catholic Church

1	2	
		Armenian-Orthodox Church
		Armenian-Catholic Church
		Coptic Church
		Lutheran Church
		Assyrian Church
		Anglican Church

1	2	
		Russian Church
		Other Denominations
		The Church of the Holy Sepulchre, place of worship of the major Christian denominations
1		The Building
2		Institution Boundary

Chapter 7　Earlier Townplanning Schemes

Earlier Townplanning Schemes

A 19th-century engraving of Jerusalem viewed from the south-east corner

The Old City

Prohibited Building Area

Restricted Building Area

Development Area

Proposed Roads

The 1918 Scheme

In December 1917, Jerusalem was occupied by the British Forces commanded by General (later Lord) Allenby. Immediately afterwards, while fighting still continued in the rest of the country and, indeed, with Turkish units still in Nablus, Allenby sent for the City Engineer of Alexandria, Mr W. McLean, to recommend a townplan for Jerusalem, bearing in mind the need to preserve the architectural traditions and historic monuments of the city. McLean's report and proposals, which were formulated in a proclamation by the Military Governor, covered the following four areas:

1 The Old City within the walls: its medieval features were to be respected. New building was to be permitted only under special conditions.

2 Areas immediately abutting the outside of the city walls: no new building was to be permitted and undesirable buildings were to be cleared. (This recommendation was not fulfilled. Only after June 1967 were the dilapidated structures, shacks and rubble in these areas removed.)

3 An area north and north-east of the Old City: building was to be allowed only with special approval and so designed as to be in harmony with the general scheme and not to conflict with the skyline of the Mount of Olives.

4 An area north and west of the Old City: this was to be the region for future development, and the plan indicated in a general way the alignment of future roads and the location of open spaces.

Within these four zones, buildings were permitted under the following conditions:

1 No building was to be placed so as to appear on the skyline of the Mount of Olives and to the south of the city.

2 No building was to be of a greater height than 11 metres above ground level.

3 Roofs were to be constructed of and covered with stone or other approved material.

4 No buildings intended for industrial purposes were to be permitted.

5 In general, approval would be given only for buildings which were an extension of the small villages embraced in this area and for special buildings to the north and west of the Old City.

This scheme was approved by the Commander-in-Chief in July 1918; the author of the scheme explained that the scheme was designed to preserve the medieval character of the Old City and to surround it by a belt of land, which should remain in its natural state as far as possible.

Source: The maps of the 1918, 1919, 1922, 1930 and 1944 Schemes are based on H. Kendall, *Jerusalem, The City Plan, 1918–1948*, London, 1948.

The 1919 Scheme

In the following year the noted scientist and town-planner Sir Patrick Geddes was invited by the Pro-Jerusalem Society to express his views on the expansion and development of Jerusalem, and he subsequently produced his plan. He, too, recommended that the Old City be surrounded by a protective belt within which building was to be restricted.

In his scheme, the road network is more flexible; the road alignment follows the topographical contours with a ring-road linking the residential quarters around the Old City. He recommended that the road network follow the natural contours. The character of the Mount of Olives to the east and the Kidron Valley to the east and south was to be preserved by designating them as a permanent open-space area. One of his major proposals which was soon put into effect concerned the siting of the projected Hebrew University. He advised that it be located on Mount Scopus, north-east of the Old City, and indeed six years later the foundation stone was laid and university buildings rose upon this superb ridge with its commanding view both of the Old City and the Dead Sea. He envisaged new building development in the then empty areas west, south-west and north-west of the Old City, and these were steadily built-up with the growing influx of Jewish immigrants following the issue of the Balfour Declaration in 1917 and the end of the war. That declaration had been issued by the British Government five weeks before the capture of Jerusalem, and its promise of the establishment of a Jewish National Home in Palestine raised high hopes among the Jewish communities of the country and the world over.

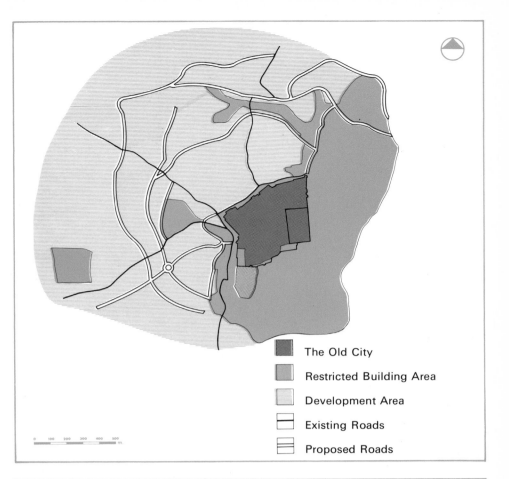

The Old City

Restricted Building Area

Development Area

Existing Roads

Proposed Roads

The 1922 Scheme

In 1921, a townplanning commission was appointed with the aim of preparing a townplanning scheme. According to this scheme, which became known as the 1922 Plan, more clearly defined zoning was proposed. The zones were to be the Old City, which was to be preserved; the protective zone of public and private open spaces around the Old City; residential and business zones; and workshops, factories and industrial zone.

For the first time, three sites for light industry were proposed near the railway station, in Bet Zefafa and in the Shneller Quarter. Thus an attempt was made to follow the quick development of the new residential quarters to the south-west and west, outside the visual space of the Old City, and the fast growth of commerce, workshops and industry in the new Jerusalem.

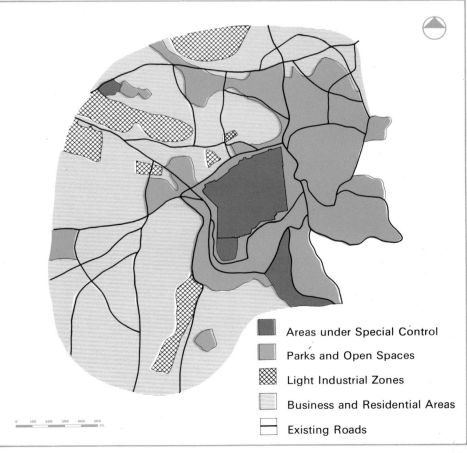

Areas under Special Control

Parks and Open Spaces

Light Industrial Zones

Business and Residential Areas

Existing Roads

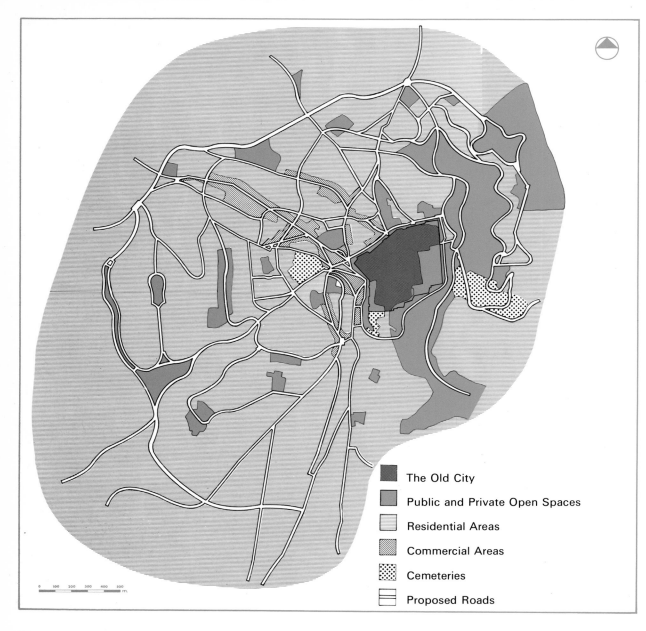

The Old City

Public and Private Open Spaces

Residential Areas

Commercial Areas

Cemeteries

Proposed Roads

600 to 1,000 square metres — and by limiting the extent of building to the main roads, and they were permitted a very much higher density by raising the maximum building percentage per plot.

Little attempt was made to earmark and secure land for parks, gardens and open spaces. The ordinance provided for only 25% of the area of a plot to be taken without compensation for public use, such as roads and gardens, and this was by no means sufficient.

On the whole, the 1930 Scheme was an important step forward in the regulative townplanning of the Jerusalem region, by dividing the area into well-defined residential, commercial and industrial zones and taking into account the needs of the growing Jewish and Arab communities in different quarters of the city.

In the 1930s and early 1940s, there was a growth in the city's population and an expansion of the new quarters outside the city walls with the rise in Jewish immigration from Nazi Germany and other European countries. With its growth, Jerusalem attracted more and more pilgrims and tourists, and it became a vibrant cosmopolitan city. Residents and visitors from all parts of the world could be seen strolling through the colourful bazaars and visiting the Holy Places of all three religions, the Via Dolorosa and the Church of the Holy Sepulchre, the Haram esh-Sharif and the Dome of the Rock, the Western Wall and the synagogues of the Jewish Quarter.

The Jews also developed their Hebrew University and Hadassah Medical Centre on Mount Scopus, as well as the new suburbs outside the city walls which they had established in the last decades of the nineteenth century. They also founded new residential suburbs to the west and south-west. The Arabs, too, started moving outside the walls and established several residential areas, particularly to the north of the Old City. The population rose steadily. In 1922, it had stood at 62,500, of whom 34,000 were Jews. In 1931, it was 90,500, of whom 51,000 were Jews. In 1947, shortly before the departure of the British, the population had grown to 117,000, of whom 97,000 were Jews.

The 1930 Scheme

In the succeeding years, an effort was made to co-ordinate the recommendations of earlier plans and incorporate them into an overall outline scheme. This was completed in 1929 and brought into force in 1930.

The principal earlier proposals concerning building restrictions in the Old City and on the Mount of Olives were maintained. The height of any new building which might be permitted within the Old City was rigidly restricted to a maximum of double the width of its skirting roadway. All building in the town was to be carried out in Jerusalem stone. The city walls were to be surrounded by a green belt, from 25 to 50 metres wide, which was to be designated as a public open space. Building within this belt was prohibited, and already-existing buildings which obstructed large sections of the ancient walls were to be removed gradually. Local authorities were granted special powers to pull down structures.

However, later on in 1935 and 1941, the Municipality, with the help of the Government and the Pro-Jerusalem Society, succeeded only in clearing the rubble from Herod's Gate and the Lions' Gate and removing the more visually offensive shops near the Damascus and Jaffa Gates. (Only after the Six Day War was the comprehensive task undertaken energetically, and the areas near the walls were cleared and planted.)

The new development areas south and south-west of the walled city were being built-up during the 1920s, and by the end of the decade they had grown to sixteen times the size of the Old City. The 1930 Scheme introduced zoning regulations for these areas, proposed a network of roads, and designated a few, relatively small, public open spaces, as well as archaeological sites which were to remain free of building. It established density control both by fixing a minimum range in the size of building plots — from

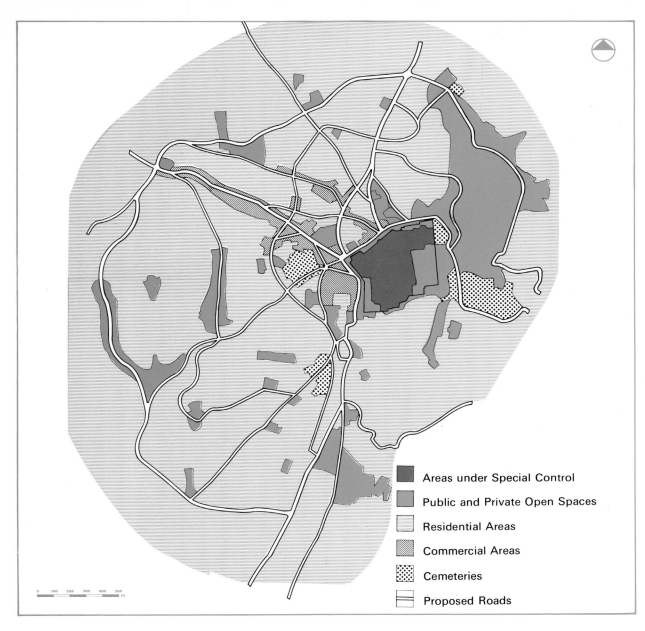

Areas under Special Control

Public and Private Open Spaces

Residential Areas

Commercial Areas

Cemeteries

Proposed Roads

construction in local stone was kept as a strict regulation for all building in Jerusalem. Exposed concrete was outlawed as being heavy, 'cold and depressing'. Drainage pipes and spouts were no longer to be installed in haphazard fashion; they had to be 'grouped together and covered by a grille' to improve the external appearance. Terraces were to be recessed and the number of balconies limited.

Open Spaces. This scheme followed the proposals in previous townplanning schemes to preserve the few remaining open spaces within the Old City, as well as protecting the Mount of Olives. Unfortunately, however, no practical steps were taken to ensure adequate open spaces for the new city suburbs. There was no recommendation for stricter legislation on rights of expropriation which would make it possible to increase the areas and the number of sites sorely needed for public buildings, gardens and parks. In many of the newly developed districts, there was considerable overcrowding, unrelieved by sufficient gardens and playgrounds.

It must be said, however, that there was little chance for the 1944 Scheme to exert a practical influence on planned development because of the rising tension in the country between Arabs, Jews and Britons. And in November 1947 came the UN Resolution which envisaged the independence of the country and the end of the British Mandate. In May 1948, the State of Israel was established and the British departed.

The 1944 Scheme

This expansion rendered the 1930 Scheme outdated, and a newly appointed townplanning adviser, Mr Henry Kendall, was asked to prepare a new plan for the city. He produced the 1944 Scheme. Whereas previous plans had dealt for the most part with the Old City and its preservation and restoration, the 1944 plan placed the main emphasis on the developing suburbs and the new areas outside the walls. The key sections of this scheme covered communications, zoning, architectural control and open spaces.

Communications. The proposals on the communications network concentrated largely on the four main highways leading into and out of Jerusalem. The Jaffa Gate was the terminal and starting point of two main roads: one to the west, to Jaffa-Tel Aviv and the Mediterranean coast, and the other to the south, to Bethlehem and Hebron. From the Damascus Gate, one highway led north to Haifa and the Galilee and

another east to Jericho. These four main arteries were connected by a ring-road which encircled the new residential suburbs of Jerusalem.

Zoning. An attempt was made to secure a tighter control over the development of the new areas by introducing ordinances relating to character, height and density. The residential suburbs outside the walls were classified into six zonal categories, with a varying minimum size of building plot and building height for each zone. The original location of the commercial zones along the principal streets and their approaches was retained; but the height of commercial building was restricted to 15 metres. It was characteristic of the optimism behind British colonial townplanning that zoning regulations were considered to be almost all that was required to secure ordered urban and architectural development.

Architectural Control. A number of ordinances were introduced which were designed to preserve or enhance the aesthetic appearance of buildings. The

131

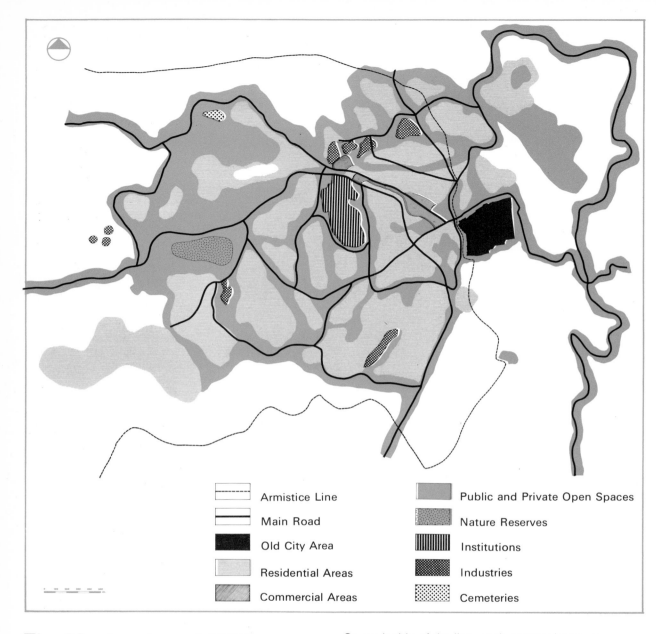

Legend:

- ‑ ‑ ‑ Armistice Line
- —— Main Road
- Old City Area
- Residential Areas
- Commercial Areas
- Public and Private Open Spaces
- Nature Reserves
- Institutions
- Industries
- Cemeteries

The Masterplan of 1950

Within hours of the proclamation of the State of Israel in 1948, the country was invaded by the regular armies of the six neighbouring Arab states. The attack on Jerusalem was particularly severe, and the Jewish community there was cut off from the rest of the Jewish population in the country. Nevertheless, morale was high, and the Jewish quarters outside the walls held their own despite the shortage of food, water, weapons and ammunition. The weak spot was the Jewish Quarter of the Old City, inhabited mostly by elderly people and surrounded by Arab attackers. On 28 May 1948 the Jewish Quarter fell. The war ended in January 1949 and the armistice lines broadly followed the cease-fire lines. In Jerusalem, the line ran roughly north to south. The area west of it, namely the whole of the new city and including Mount Zion, came within Israel. The area to its east, including the Old City, fell under Jordanian control. Jerusalem became a divided city.

On each side of the line, each country began to develop its part of Jerusalem. The Jordanians continued to expand their suburbs beyond the city walls, again mostly to the north. The development of Israeli Jerusalem was infinitely greater, since the need was greater; for this was the period when the vast influx of immigrants was at its peak, and a complex of new residential suburbs soon sprang up, spreading ever westwards.

During the first decade of the state, a number of impressive public buildings were also erected. The most important were the new Hebrew University campus on Givat Ram, the National Library and a huge sports stadium; more recent additions were the new Knesset (Parliament) building, the Israel Museum with its art pavilions, open-air sculpture garden and the Shrine of the Book housing the Dead Sea Scrolls. This development was guided by the Jerusalem Masterplan of 1950, prepared by the National Planning Authority of the Prime Minister's Office. Under the Mandatory Government, the town schemes

were concerned mostly with regulative planning, whereas in the 1950 Masterplan there was an attempt to find an organic solution for the different urban problems and at the same time have the city serve the main functions as capital of Israel and as spiritual fount. Provision therefore had to be made for its development as a political, cultural and religious centre with a firm economic base, providing for the establishment of light industries and the development of tourism, trade and handicrafts.

The area covered by the Masterplan was 38,000 dunams, 60% larger than the municipal area within Israel's boundaries at the time. It envisaged a future population of more than 200,000, which was double the figure at that time. The following is a brief outline of the 1950 Masterplan's principal features:

Residential Areas. The Judean hills south-west and west of the city were well suited as a pleasant and healthy location for a residential zone and should be added to the municipal area. These hills, the same height as Jerusalem, would constitute natural neighbourhood units and accentuate the setting of the city as a mountain capital in their midst.

Commercial and Industrial Areas. The plan provided for a commercial centre within the city and industrial zones in the outskirts. This would require the reconstruction of the city centre, which would not be difficult as only a small number of the buildings were financially valuable. To reduce congestion, it was proposed that the commercial area be limited by the laying out of a park round the Mamilla Pool and its nearby antiquities.

The Government Centre (the Kirya). Several hills round Givat Ram, west of the Old City and now at the centre of new Jerusalem, were expropriated and designated as the location of the future buildings of the Knesset, the new campus of the University and the government ministries. This high ground overlooks the entire region. It would be surrounded by a green belt linking it to Mount Herzl and the Hadassah Medical Centre in the west.

Communications. The plan envisaged a network of communications suited to the mountainous terrain. Two main roads, running west and south, were to link the capital with the rest of the country. They would join the outer circular road at the western entrance to the city, and from this point there would be direct access to all parts of the city, as well as to the inner ring serving the Kirya.

Parks and Open Spaces. One of the most important parts of the plan was the proposal to establish a green belt serving the entire city. The topography of Jerusalem offers a natural solution to this problem. All *wadis,* ravines and valleys between the hills on which the city stands could serve as a network of gardens and parks, a sequence of green strips separating the neighbourhood units. The centre of the green belt would be Mount Herzl, a steep hill west of the city commanding a superb view of the Judean wilderness to the east and the coastal plain to the west. The green belt would continue until it reaches the proposed National Park area of over 90,000 dunams in the afforested Judean Hills.

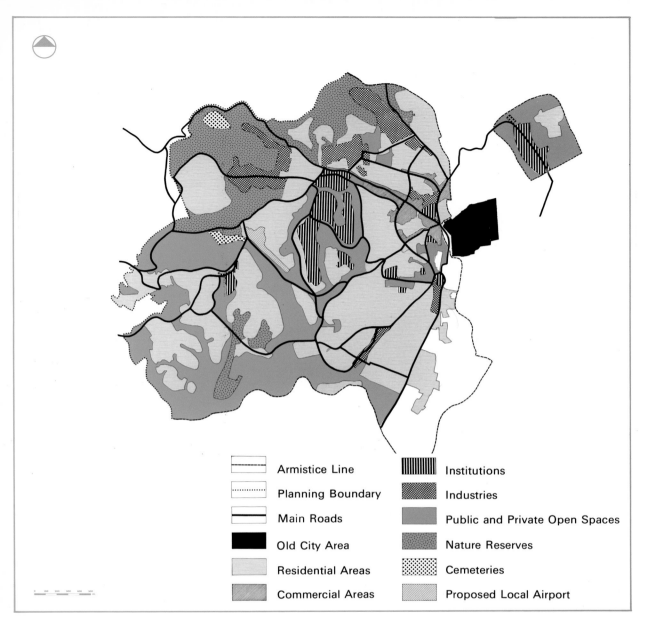

☰ Armistice Line	▥ Institutions
⋯ Planning Boundary	▦ Industries
═ Main Roads	▨ Public and Private Open Spaces
■ Old City Area	▦ Nature Reserves
░ Residential Areas	▦ Cemeteries
▨ Commercial Areas	▨ Proposed Local Airport

The 1959 Scheme

This scheme was prepared by the planning authority of the Ministry of the Interior in 1957 and finally approved by the local and district townplanning commissions in 1959.

In its basic planning conception, it broadly followed the original guidelines laid down in the 1950 Masterplan for Jerusalem, taking into account the new residential units, the government centre, the Hebrew University campus and the Hadassah Medical Centre — buildings which had risen in the meantime in accordance with the general outline of the Masterplan. The basic features of the 1959 Scheme were:

Residential Neighbourhoods. The residential quarters in the east and centre of the town, which for the most part were too densely populated, were subject to reconstruction and renovation based on detailed plans. The western part of the town, adjoining the then built-up area, consists of a number of hills and each was planned as a compact neighbourhood unit, with commercial and educational centres and craftsmen and artisans' services for each unit. The remaining open spaces — for the most part steep slopes and valleys — were designated as green open spaces to serve the immediate neighbourhoods. This ring of built-up hills with open spaces in the ravines in between was to give the suburbs of Jerusalem their special character.

Industry. The industrial zones were to be limited to light industry, requiring less raw material and therefore no bulky transport, but a high degree of skill. They were located mainly in the north of the town, at Romema, Givat Shaul, Sanhedria and in an additional area in the south; it was estimated that the existing and projected industrial zones would be sufficient for the needs of an envisaged population of 200,000 in the future.

Communications. The inter-urban roads — the Old Jaffa Road and the Security Road entering the city near Ramat Raziel — were marked in accordance with the Regional Plan. Main traffic arteries between the various quarters, connecting roads and additional approaches from the south of the city to the north, by-passing the existing centre, were also planned. A central bus station and parking lots were marked on the plan.

Building Regulations. The by-laws requiring the facing of buildings to be carried out in natural, local stone were kept in force. However, in view of the high cost of public housing schemes, the zones to which this regulation applied had to be reduced. The city was therefore divided into building zones of natural stone, artificial stone, and concrete with stucco finish in the suburbs.

The main civic, cultural and administrative centre was located in Romema, near the newly built National Convention Centre. Romema lies right at the western entrance to the city, near the main roads leading to the new and old town. It was chosen mainly because of its high altitude and its commanding view over the entire vicinity.

.The government centre, the University campus, the Knesset and the Israel Museum near the deep Valley of the Cross, with its monastery, were located on a hilly chain, Givat Ram, overlooking the south and adjacent to the Romema Centre. Their construction started along the guidelines of the 1950 Masterplan, and together they form a complex of public buildings closely related to the green gardens around them.

The hilly landscape west of the city extends from Givat Ram, site of the Hebrew University campus and the Israel Museum, to the green hills of Mount Herzl, the Yad Vashem Memorial for the victims of the Nazi holocaust and onwards to the Hadassah Medical Centre perched on a hillock near Ein Karem. All *wadis*, valleys and rifts lying between these hills were to form a network of gardens, parks and open fields, linking up with the National Park in the mountains of Judea in the extreme west.

Jerusalem Master Plan 1968

The 1968 Jerusalem masterplan is a development plan for the Jerusalem area. It was presented in two parts: a plan for the immediate conditions (the 1986 Plan) and two alternate plans for future considerations (the 2010 Plan). The authors of of the plan, the architect-planners, Prof. A. Hashimshony, Joseph Schweid and Zion Hashimshony, based the plan on the assumption of organic interrelation between three urban entities: (1) the historic nucleus which includes the Old City of Jerusalem, the Mount of Olives and a surrounding park system (2) the continuous, highly populated urban ring which spreads around the historical center up to a well-defined verge and (3) a metropolitan area which includes low-density residential areas, agricultural settlements, small townships (Bethlehem and Ramalla) and especially vast nature reserves.

The general aims of the plan were:

1   To establish an urban structure for a unified city, freely accessible both locally and internationally, functionally suitable as the capital of the State of Israel, as a world-wide spiritual and cultural centre and as a dignified home for its varied groups of residents, permanent and transitory.

2   To ensure the preservation and enhancement of the historical treasures and landscape.

The plan was examined for its adaptability to conditions that may prevail at the end of the century.

The plan re-adopted several principles common to previous plans, which were prepared for the city as a whole. These are: the preservation of the Old City, the establishment of a park surrounding the Old City and the use of stone as a cladding material for buildings.

The general layout consists of four zones, the innermost being the historic nucleus surrounded by a park covering the valleys of Jehoshaphat and Hinnom and the Mount of Olives and extending eastward into the Judean Desert. The second zone forms the internal city, containing within its boundaries the government centre, educational, religious and cultural institutions and central commercial and social facilities. The third, mostly residential zone comprises the city proper to its verge — a belt of open landscape which separates the compactly built city from the metropolitan area and prevents the continuous sprawl of the city. The fourth zone includes the entire metropolitan area with its various settlements.

A view of the Judean Desert from the Mount of Olives

Out of the 110 sq.km. of municipal area 36.5 sq.km. were in use in 1967. It is assumed that 26 sq.km. of the unused land will be developed in 1985. The 1967 breakdown of land use and the assumed increases are listed below:

LAND USE	Area in 1967 (sq.km.)	Assumed increase by 1985 (sq.km.)
Residential (net)	11.2	4.0
Commercial	0.8	1.0
Governmental	0.5	1.0
Public Utilities	1.5	0.0
Public Institutions	4.1	4.0
Industrial	0.7	1.0
Public Open Space	4.0	10.0
Cemeteries	0.8	1.0
Agricultural	8.1	−2.0
Roads (arterial & local)	4.8	6.0
Total	36.5	26.0

The plan indicates areas for renewal and reorganises the functional structure, balancing the distribution of employment and residential population. The special character of Jerusalem is expressed by the growth of the area allocated to public uses.

The planned road network is a modification of the existing road structure, allowing the efficient linking of the entire city by a public transportation system and answering the needs arising from increasing motorisation. It is designed for easy orientation and calls for the development of environmental units within it. The arterial road system is composed of: (1) a primary net which is a continuation of the historic roads leading to the town. These roads, which historically converged on the Old City, were shifted to the brink of the central urban complexes, serving them tangentially. (2)   A secondary net within the city takes the form of an orthogonal grid, spaced according to the requirements of an efficient bus service. A proposed central boulevard connects the major foci of the city: the university on Mount Scopus, the Mount of Olives, the Old City, the central area, the government centre and Mount Herzl.

The outline scheme prepared for the Old City and its environs, which formulates the planning regulations with special emphasis on the strict visual control of this sensitive area, was prepared in coordination with the masterplan and its basic conception.

A set of recommendations forms a disciplinary
framework which will maintain and enhance the
cultural and visual image of the city:

1 Preservation of sites having cultural or visual
   value listed in an inventory attached to the plan,
   with special emphasis on the historic nucleus.
2 Continuation of the by-law requiring stone
   cladding for all buildings.
3 Reintroduction of the traditional street as an
   organising element of the city's texture.
4 Strict control of building heights within the
   visual basin of the Old City.
5 Proper treatment of the entrances to the city.
6 Provision of a belt of open landscape separating
   the city from the metropolitan settlements,
   providing a visually clear definition of the city
   and an appropriate design of its verge.

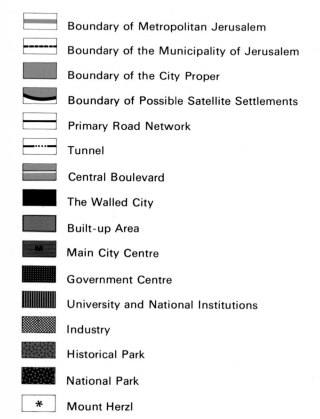

Boundary of Metropolitan Jerusalem

Boundary of the Municipality of Jerusalem

Boundary of the City Proper

Boundary of Possible Satellite Settlements

Primary Road Network

Tunnel

Central Boulevard

The Walled City

Built-up Area

Main City Centre

Government Centre

University and National Institutions

Industry

Historical Park

National Park

Mount Herzl

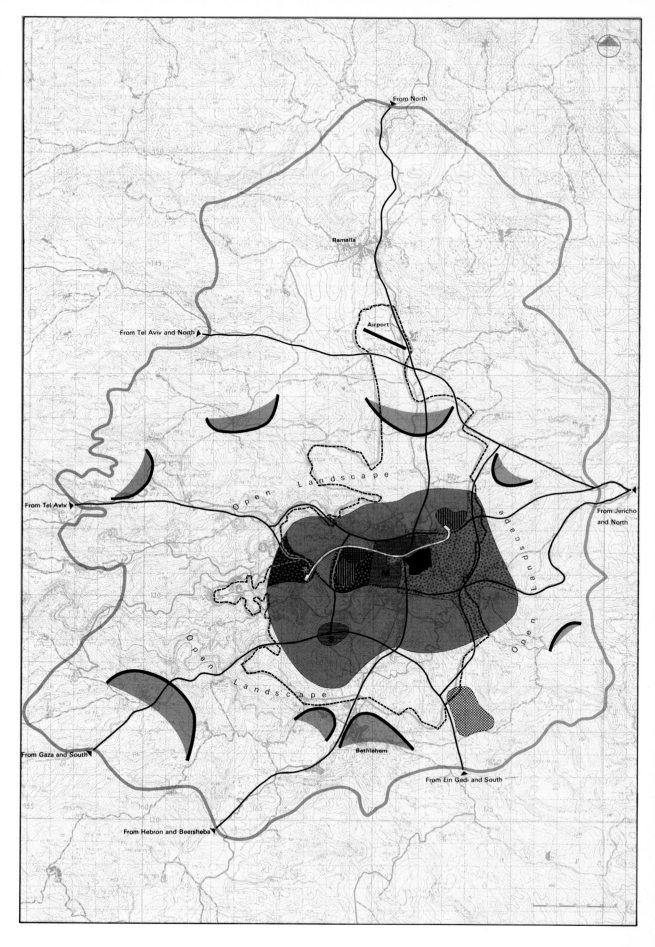

136

Chapter 8　The Outline Scheme of the Special Zone

The Outline Scheme of the Special Zone

The proposed Outline Scheme seeks to present the general lines along which the area of the Special Zone — the Old City and its environs — should be developed, taking into account its basic physical and socio-economic conditions. It is also inspired by the specific purpose of preserving the special character of a zone composed of unique historical, architectural and landscape values. The planning and development aims for this area are proposed as part of the overall masterplan for the united city of Jerusalem.

The area covered by the Outline Scheme of the Special Zone is roughly 10,500 dunams (10.5 square kilometres) and covers only 10% of the over 100,000 dunams (100 sq. km.) of the Greater Jerusalem townplanning area. The location of the Special Zone is peripheral to the Greater Jerusalem area, but its city centres lie close by, to the north-west, near the Old City between the Jaffa Gate and the Damascus Gate. The main residential quarters of Jerusalem are located to the south-west and north-west of these centres and contain larger resources of land still not built upon and suitable for additional residential neighbourhoods and industrial zones, which could be developed easily together with the city's growth. There is no practical need or demand to enlarge the population of the Special Zone to any considerable extent.

The immediate function of the scheme was to determine and regulate the usage of the land within the zone: to demarcate the residential areas, both existing and projected, and prescribe the maximum density and height of their buildings; to designate special sites for religious, cultural and social institutions, public buildings, hotels and pilgrim centres; to preserve areas for archaeological excavations, public open spaces, gardens, parks and nature reserves; and to provide for a variety of public services, including a network of roads, to be co-ordinated with the communications' masterplan for the entire city.

A comprehensive survey of the entire area was undertaken, and some of the results of this basic study are presented in a series of survey maps, showing population data and density, land use, landscape values, the existing communication network, built-up areas and sites and structures of special historical and architectural value. (See maps on following pages.) Based on specific surveys of the Old City, its environs and immediate neighbourhoods, the study of its physical background, historical past, social and economic conditions, its architecture and landscape values, the Outline Scheme comprises the following main features:

The Outline Scheme provides the basis for the preparation of detailed schemes for the different parts of the zone. The area has accordingly been subdivided into twenty units (see map 1), so that the detailed planning of each can proceed more or less independently The 'boundaries' of the units were determined by such factors as natural topographic features, roads, land usage (both existing and proposed), land ownership and demography.

A view of the Old City from the Russian Tower on the Mount of Olives

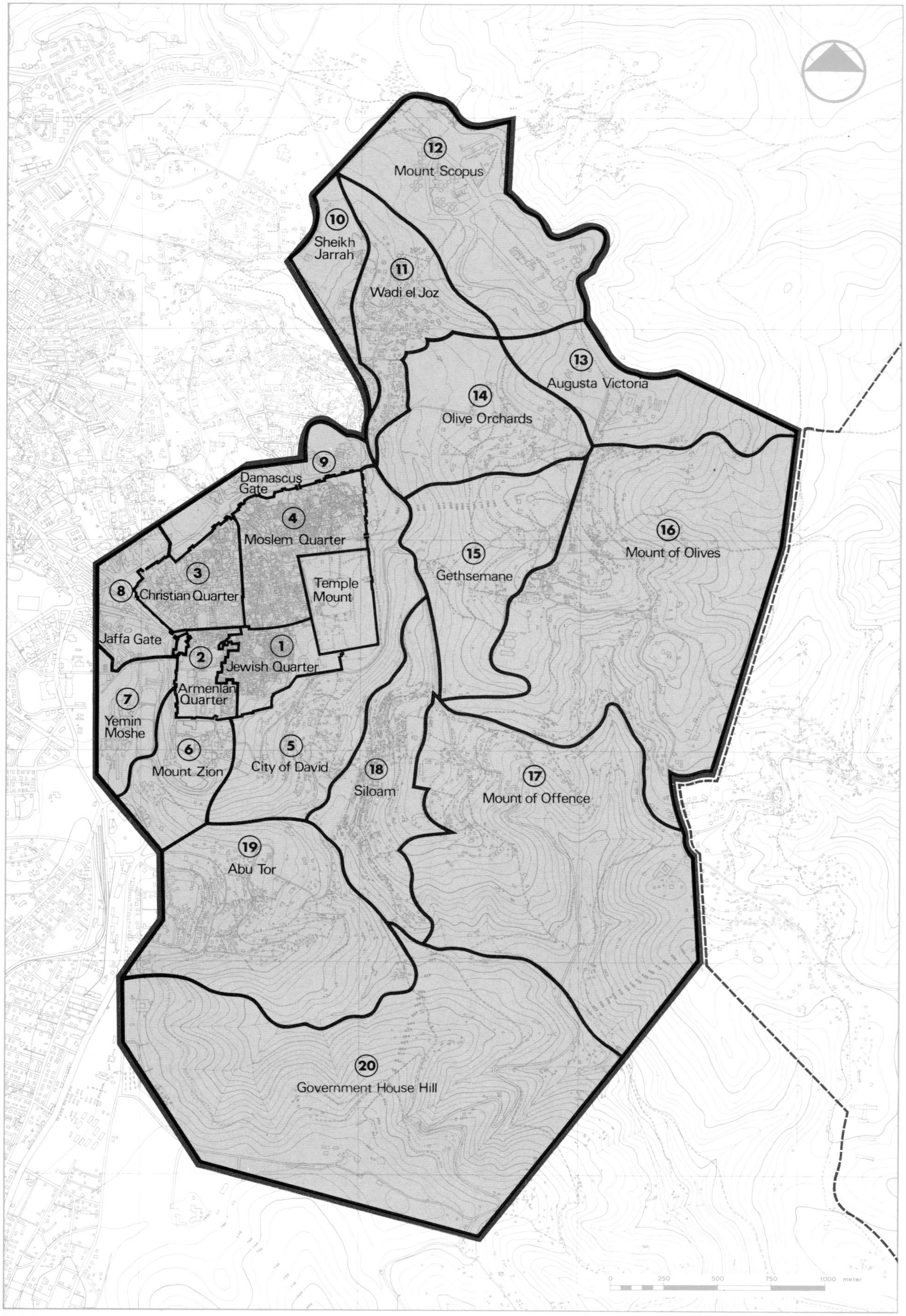

Subunits–Detailed Schemes

The detailed schemes for the sub-units will be guided by three maps attached to the Outline Scheme. Map 11 indicates the most attractive areas which are recommended as worthy of preservation. Map 13 gives the topography of the zone, with its special townscape and landscape features. Map 14 shows the dominating skyline of the area — the ridges — as well as the valleys that lie between the hills and the city. Indicated on this map are observation points and touring routes which are not only themselves impressive but also afford impressive views. The Mount of Olives, for example, commands the most magnificent view of the Old City, as well as of the Kidron Valley at its foot and the Jordan Valley, the Dead Sea and the mountains of Moab in the distance. Map 15 gives the location of all the historical and religious sites and the buildings of special architectural significance within the Special Zone. (For a detailed map of the Old City, see page 123.)

Boundary of Planning Area

Municipal Boundary

Boundary of Planning Units

Number of Planning Unit

2

Relief Model of Special Zone

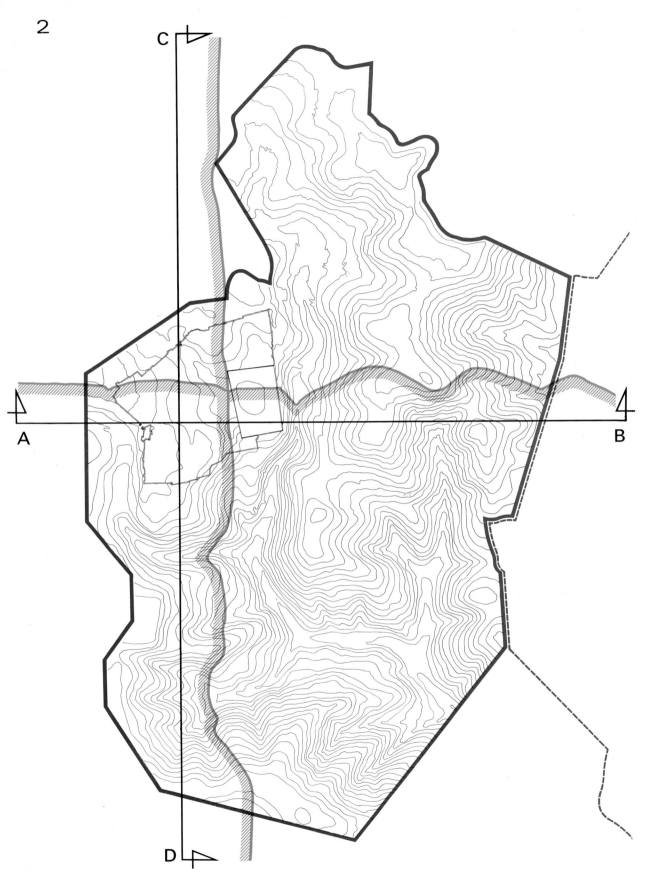

Relief Map of Special Zone.
Red lines indicate topographic cross-
sections A-B and C-D

141

*Undulating, terraced hill structure around
the Old City*

Steepness of Gradients

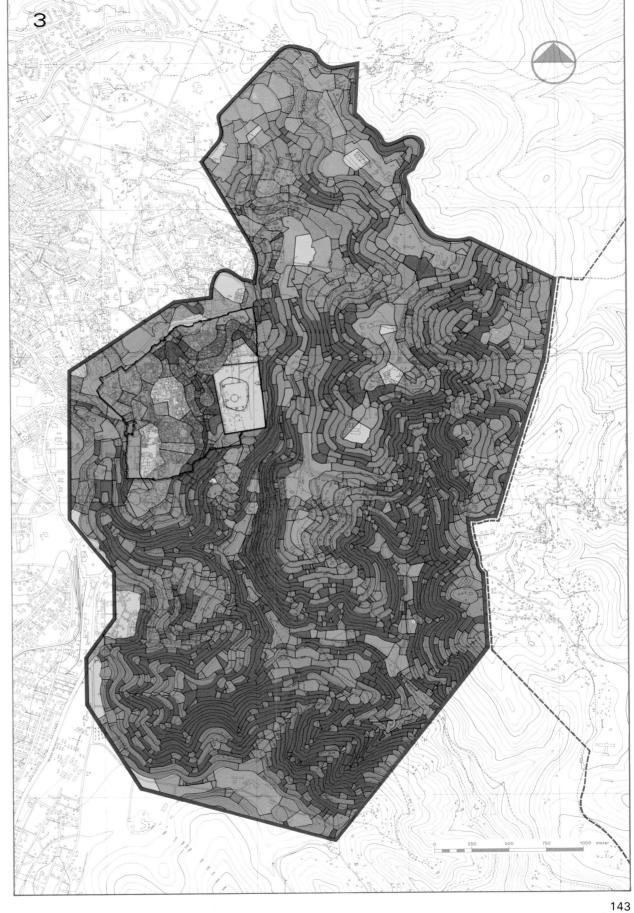

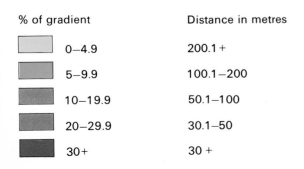

% of gradient	Distance in metres
0–4.9	200.1+
5–9.9	100.1–200
10–19.9	50.1–100
20–29.9	30.1–50
30+	30 +

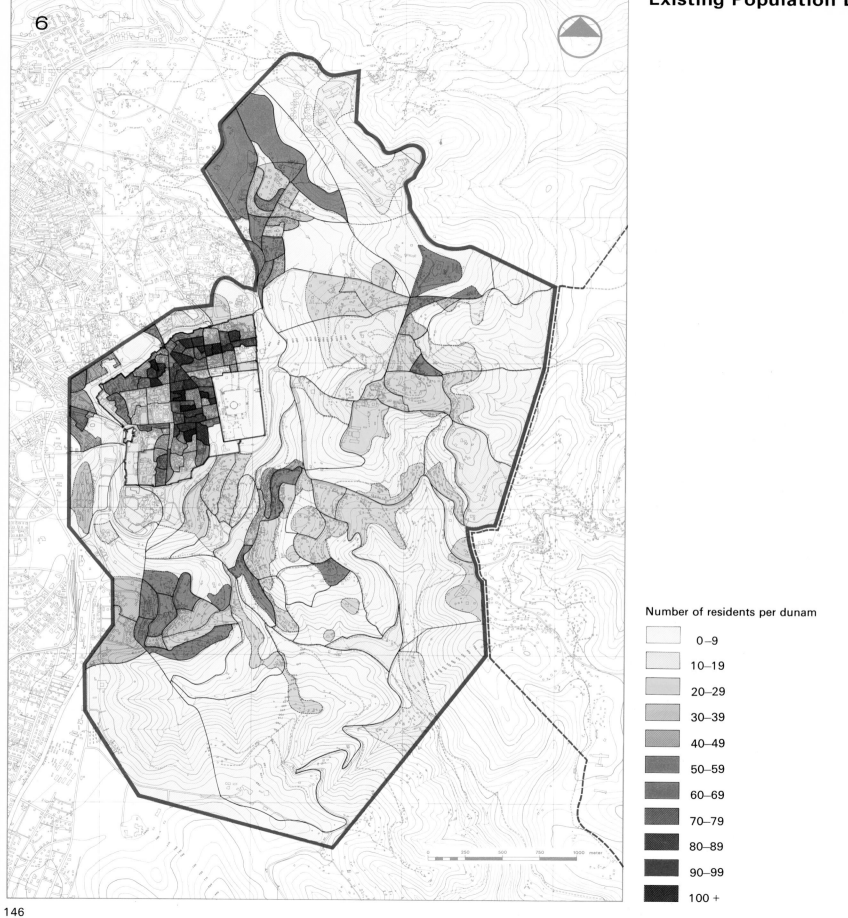

Existing Population Density

Number of residents per dunam

	0–9
	10–19
	20–29
	30–39
	40–49
	50–59
	60–69
	70–79
	80–89
	90–99
	100 +

0   250   500   750   1000 meter

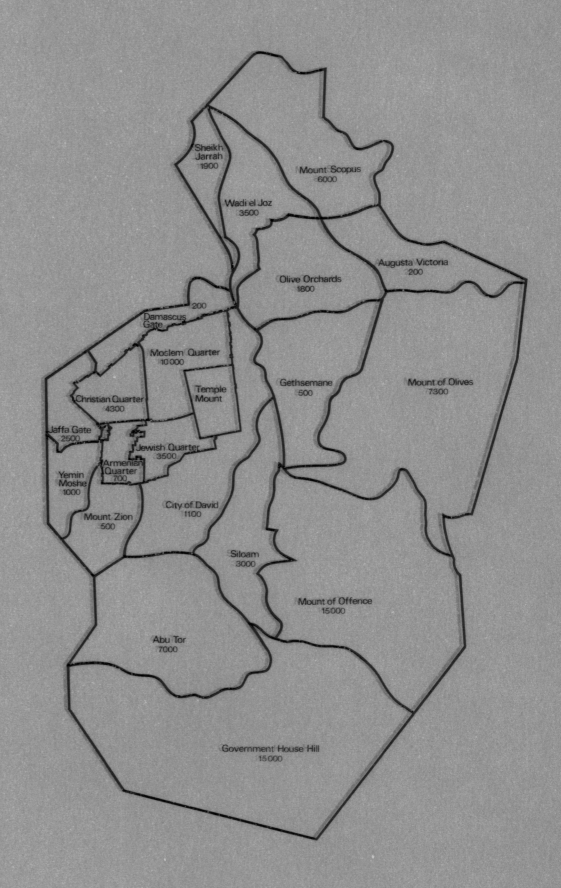

Sheikh
Jarrah
1900

Mount Scopus
6000

Wadi el Joz
3500

Augusta Victoria
200

Olive Orchards
1800

200

Damascus
Gate

Moslem Quarter
10000

Temple
Mount

Gethsemane
500

Mount of Olives
7300

Christian Quarter
4300

Jaffa Gate
2500

Jewish Quarter
3500

Armenian
Quarter
700

Yemin
Moshe
1000

City of David
1100

Mount Zion
500

Siloam
3000

Mount of Offence
15000

Abu Tor
7000

Government House Hill
15000

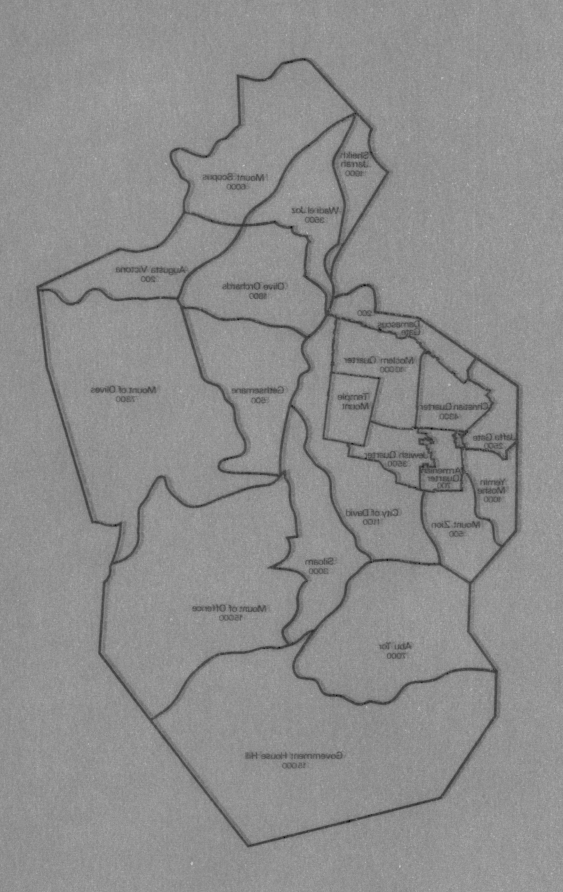

Proposed Population Density

The proposed residential capacity of the zone is approximately 85,000 inhabitants, as compared to the total of 55,000 who live there now. As indicated earlier, the main residential area now within the zone is located inside the Old City, which holds 24,000 inhabitants, and the planners have recommended that the number should not exceed 20,000. Further residential units are planned as extensions of the existing ones: Abu-Tor with about 7,000 inhabitants, Siloam and the Mount of Offence with 18,000, Government House Hill with roughly 15,000 inhabitants and Mount Scopus with its student population of about 10,000. The proposed population capacity may be even lower due to the intention of the Jerusalem Municipality to increase the open-space areas and to lower the population density on the southern hills. Large-scale and organic residential projects for the fast-growing population of the Greater Jerusalem area are planned south-west and north of the former municipal boundaries (see 1968 Master-plan, page 135).

Almost all the residential areas outside the Old City walls considered by the scheme are those which already exist, such as the neighbourhoods of Abu-Tor, North Talpiot, Wadi Jos, and A-Tur on the Mount of Olives. Additional residential quarters have been proposed south-east of Siloam village, on the slopes of the Mount of Offence and on the north-eastern slope of Government House Hill. These sites, which lie outside the amphitheatre setting of the Old City and do not compete with it, are intended to serve primarily those persons relocated from the slum quarters of the Old City and also those whose dwellings are on land required for widening roads or marked for archaeological excavation. Additional low-density residential quarters, interspersed by public open spaces, were proposed on the northern slope of Government House Hill, which is included in the Outline Scheme area. However, Government House Hill as a whole will be subject to an integral and comprehensive architectural plan with particular emphasis on its northern slopes. For it is this slope which overlooks the Old City and the National Park near the valleys of Hinnom and Kidron, and it is therefore of special architectural and landscape value.

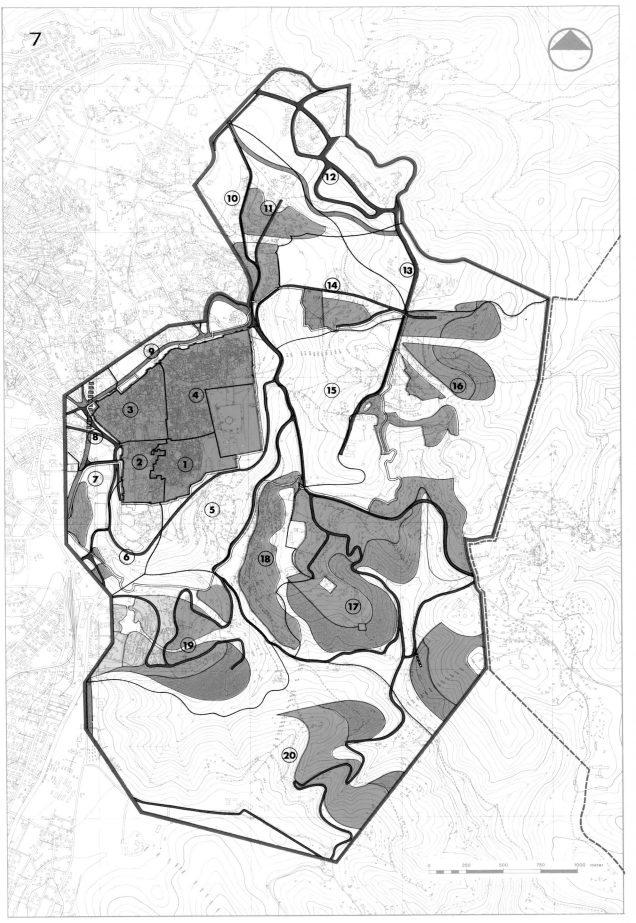

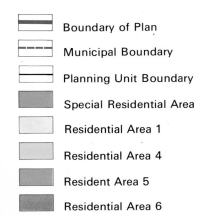

Boundary of Plan

Municipal Boundary

Planning Unit Boundary

Special Residential Area

Residential Area 1

Residential Area 4

Resident Area 5

Residential Area 6

Built-up Area

The scheme pinpoints the overcrowded slum areas in the Old City, which are in urgent need of rehabilitation, and proposes, as the only additional residential sector inside the city, the restoration of the Jewish Quarter, which was destroyed in 1948. Additional reconstruction areas in the Special Zone are the picturesque Siloam village, south-east of the Old City, and the Yemin Moshe Quarter. The one- and two-storey houses built in local stone are of homogeneous shape and scale and are well suited to the gentle slopes and terraced sites. But many of the buildings are derelict and desolate, and the two neighbourhoods are in sore need of reconstruction. It is difficult to impose normal building by-laws for these areas — with the exception of by-laws governing building height and prescribing the use of local stone. Therefore, the scheme calls for careful architectural control of all building activities within these areas, which should be co-ordinated and inspected by special architectural committees.

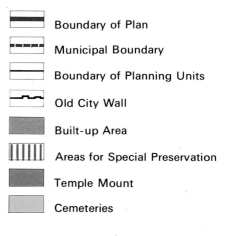

Boundary of Plan	
Municipal Boundary	
Boundary of Planning Units	
Old City Wall	
Built-up Area	
Areas for Special Preservation	
Temple Mount	
Cemeteries	

Open Spaces

The natural topography and microlandscape dictated the alignment of the open spaces in the Special Zone. The problem and its solution were clear and almost preconditioned. The deep valleys of Hinnom and Kidron constitute the obvious basic features of the open-space network. They are to be preserved, together with the low, dried-up riverbeds. The climbing rocky slopes, partly covered by ancient cemeteries, are to be planted or reforested. Their terracing, where already disintegrated, must be renewed. The slopes of the Siloam village, Yemin Moshe Quarter and the Mount of Olives should be carefully preserved. All these areas are part of the National Park already approved by the government. This park area is connected by green strips or wider valleys — designated by the scheme as public or private open spaces — with the steep ravines and barren hills in the east overlooking the Dead Sea and the Jericho plain and with the mountains of Moab in the background. The scheme seeks to connect the National Park area around the Old City with the built-up areas in the north-west and south-west by green strips, tree or flower-lined avenues and foot-paths, thus ensuring a green open-space network throughout the planning area of Greater Jerusalem.

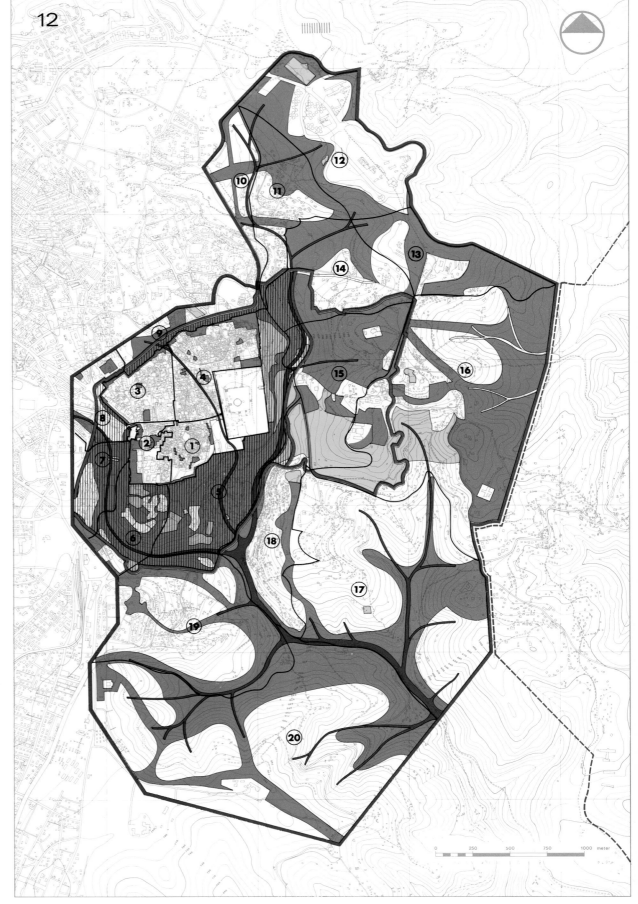

Boundary of Plan

Municipal Boundary

Valley

Open Spaces

Cemeteries

National Park Boundaries

Proposed Boundary

Approved Boundary

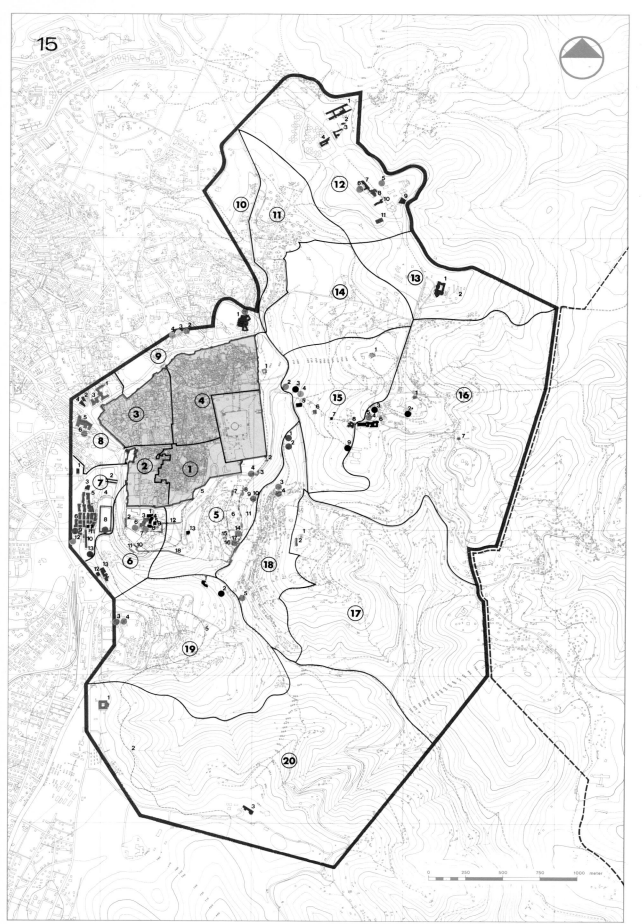

Location of Historical, Religious and Architectural Sites

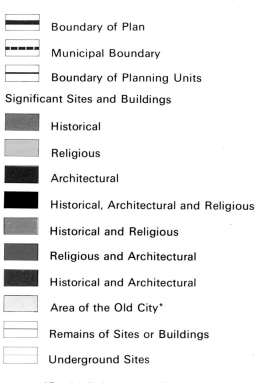

Boundary of Plan

Municipal Boundary

Boundary of Planning Units

Significant Sites and Buildings

Historical

Religious

Architectural

Historical, Architectural and Religious

Historical and Religious

Religious and Architectural

Historical and Architectural

Area of the Old City*

Remains of Sites or Buildings

Underground Sites

0   250   500   750   1000 meter

*For detailed scheme of Old City, see page 123.

Planning Unit No. 5 – City of David

- 1 St Mary's Pool
- 2 Ophel Wall
- 3 Tower in the Ophel Wall
- 4 Kenyon Excavations in Zone S
- 5 Aqueduct from Second Temple Period
- 6 City of David
- 7 The Valley Gate from First Temple Period
- 8 Hasmonean Tower and Nehemiah's Wall
- 9 Jebusite Water-supply Shaft
- 10 The Virgin's Fountain (Gihon Spring)
- 11 Hezekiah's Tunnel
- 12 Eastern Wall of Upper City
- 13 St Peter in Gallicantu
- 14 Probable Royal Tombs of the Jewish Monarchy
- 15 Siloam Church and Mosque of Siloam
- 16 Siloam Pool
- 17 Tomb in City of David
- 18 Southern City Wall from Second Temple Period

Planning Unit No. 6 – Mount Zion

- 1 Armenian House of Caiaphas and St Saviour
- 2 Bishop Gobat School
- 3 Church of the Dormition
- 4 Caenaculum
- 5 Synagogue – House of Testament
- 6 Excavations on Mount Zion
- 7 Mosque of the Prophet David
- 8 David's Tomb
- 9 Holocaust Cellar
- 10 South City Wall from Second Temple Period
- 11 Aqueduct, Second Temple Period
- 12 Jerusalem House of Quality
- 13 Knights of St Johns' Quarter

Planning Unit No. 7 – Yemin Moshe Quarter

- 1 French Consulate
- 2 Huzot Hayozer – Artisans' Arcade
- 3 Former St George Convent
- 4 Aqueduct from the Second Temple Period
- 5 Yemin Moshe Quarter
- 6 Gate and First House in Yemin Moshe
- 7 The Sephardi Synagogue
- 8 Sultan's Pool and Fountain (water fountain)
- 9 Sir Moses Montefiore Memorial – Windmill
- 10 Judah Touro Dwellings
- 11 Cistern
- 12 Quarry near Mishkenoth Sha'ananim Quarter
- 13 Peace Memorial

Planning Unit No. 8 – Jaffa Gate

- 1 Notre Dame de France
- 2 Missionary Building
- 3 Louis French Hospital
- 4 Townhall
- 5 St Vincent de Paul Hospice
- 6 Room Where Herzl Stayed (1898)

Planning Unit No. 9 – Damascus Gate

- 1 Palestine Archaeological Museum
- 2 Jeremiah's Cave
- 3 El-Zahirah Hill (Gordon's Calvary)
- 4 Garden Tomb
- 5 Parachuters' Memorial

Planning Unit No. 12 – Mount Scopus

- 1 Hadassah Hospital
- 2 Former Administrative Building
- 3 Former Hadassah Nurses' College
- 4 Ratnof Medical Institute
- 5 Nicanor's Cave
- 6 Burial Cave
- 7 Rosenblum College for Judaic Studies
- 8 National and University Library
- 9 Amphitheatre
- 10 Museum of Jewish Antiquities

Planning Unit No. 13 – Augusta Victoria

- 1 Augusta Victoria Hospital
- 2 Dr Calahan's House

Planning Unit No. 15 – Gethsemane

- 1 Viri Galilaei Church
- 2 Parachuters' Memorial
- 3 Church of the Assumption or Tomb of the Virgin
- 4 Grotto of Gethsemane
- 5 Church of All Nations or Basilica of Agony
- 6 St Mary Magdalene Church
- 7 Church of Dominus Flevit Convent
- 8 Benedictine Monastery
- 9 The Prophets' Tombs

Planning Unit No. 16 – Mount of Olives

- 1 Suleiman El-Parsi Minaret
- 2 Russian Compound
- 3 Church of the Ascension
- 4 El-Asadia Minaret
- 5 Tomb of the Santa Pelagia
- 6 Carmelite Convent and Pater Noster Church
- 7 Bethphage Monastery

Planning Unit No. 17 – Mount of Offence

- 1 Syrian Catholic Patriarchate
- 2 Benedictine Monastery – Maison d'Abraham

Planning Unit No. 18 – Siloam

- 1 Tomb of Jehosafat and Absalom's Pillar
- 2 St James' Tomb and Zechariah's Tomb
- 3 Tomb of Pharaoh's Daughter
- 4 Tomb of . . . yahu
- 5 Ein-Rogel

Planning Unit No. 19 – Abu-Tor

- 1 Haceldama
- 2 Burial Caves
- 3 Sheik's Tomb
- 4 Remains of Byzantine Church
- 5 Aqueduct from the Second Temple Period

Planning Unit No. 20 – Hill of Evil Counsel (Government House Hill)

- 1 Convent of the Poor Clares
- 2 Aqueduct from the Second Temple Period
- 3 Government House

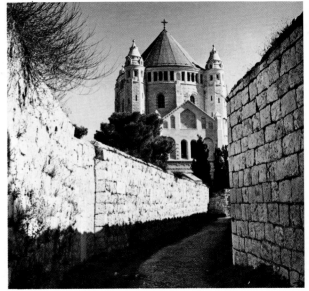

For Planning units Nos. 1, 2, 3, 4 see detailed scheme of Old City, page 123

The Outline Scheme of the Special Zone

With the implementation of the proposals presented in the scheme for the completion of existing neighbourhoods and the building up of new areas, the great problem arises of how to preserve this landscape, how to safeguard the existing homogeneous building character, how to continue the new buildings without imitating conventional shapes and styles of the past.

To be sure, the scheme imposes certain basic requirements and by-laws, such as use of local stone for new residential buildings or larger stone panels for higher public buildings; regulations controlling building sites, building ratio and building height and a general recommendation for the detailed schemes, to keep the one- to two-storey buildings on the lower slopes near the valleys and the higher buildings climbing up the slopes, while the ridges are reserved for public buildings surrounded by gardens and open spaces. All these are important measures to regulate building habits and impose a certain discipline under careful consideration of the visual silhouette along the hill ridges. These regulations will naturally direct the authors of the detailed schemes, serving as basic design guidelines, but they are not sufficient to ensure positive and valuable architectural solutions. We have learned a sad lesson from several buildings erected during the Jordanian rule (public buildings and hotels) which are damaging for their environment even though they are executed in local stone and in the pattern of conventional arches and domes.

The positive and definite results depend on a sound and architectural approach, which should be comprehensive for every building compound and for the whole neighbourhood. A single building, even if it has good architectural qualities, is only of small importance for the townscape as a whole. The architectural challenge for a comprehensive solution is to prepare the detailed schemes, with a basic architectural idea regarding space entity and space relationship to the surrounding landscape and townscape and to find a strong and effective architectural team which would follow the general idea and execute it to the last details. The specific architectural assets of Jerusalem landscape and townscape, and the historic values of this area, call for architectural high quality, comprehensiveness and unity.

The proposed residential areas on the northern slopes of Government House Hill, the south-eastern part of Abu-Tor and the Mount of Offence, and the western slopes of the Abu Dis Hill (lying south of the broken line on map 16) were finally designated by the Ministry of Interior and the Municipality of Jerusalem as a special area for future planning, with the purpose of reducing densities of residential quarters and providing for more public open spaces in the detailed architectural schemes to be prepared in the future.

Boundary of Plan

Municipal Boundary

Planning Unit Boundary

Old City Area*

Area for Detailed Planning

Preservation and Restoration Area

Area Reserved for Archaeological Excavations

Archaeological Site

Special Residential Area

Residential Area 1

Residential Area 4

Residential Area 5

Residential Area 6

Area for Institutions

Area for Hotels, Recreation and Institutions

Public Buildings Area

Commercial Area

National Park Boundary

Public Open Space Area

Public Open Space for Detailed Planning

Private Open Space

Sport and Recreation Area

Cemetery

Proposed Cemetery

Proposed Main Road

Existing Road

*For detailed scheme of Old City, see page 123.

1 Name of the Plan

This plan is to be known as 'The Outline Plan for Jerusalem (The Old City and Environs)', Townplanning Scheme No. AM-9, hereafter 'The Scheme'.

2 Delineation of the Scheme

The blue boundary on the attached map indicated the boundary of the area to which the plan applies.

3 Drawings of the Scheme

A plan of the Old City and Environs at a scale of 1:5,000, and a detailed plan of the Old City within the walls at a scale of 1:2,500.

4 Nature of the Scheme

4.1 The regulations of the Scheme will be identical with the regulations appearing in the Outline Plan, as gazzetted in Bulletin No. 1359, dated 11.9.44, and subsequent changes as approved in the Townplanning Scheme No. 62 gazzetted in Bulletin No. 687-p, dated 16.7.59, called hereafter Outline Plan No. 62, except in cases where explicitly indicated otherwise in the Plan (regulations and drawing).

5 Interpretation of Terms

Terms not detailed in these regulations are to be interpreted according to the Outline Plan No. 62.

6 Objects of the Scheme

6.1 To allow for the development of the area to which the scheme relates, while carefully preserving its special character.
6.2 To determine the various land zoning and the permitted uses of land and buildings; the alignment of the main arterial road system; to determine the form of building, all as described in these regulations.
6.3 To serve as a basis for the preparation of Detailed Townplanning Schemes for this area.
6.4 To preserve the natural landscape and townscape within the area of the Scheme.
6.5 To guard the traditional sites and Holy Places.

7 Subdivision into Areas

7.1 *Legend:* Parts of the legend not detailed in these regulations will be considered as the interpretation given in the Outline Plan No. 62.

Description of Legend		Definition of Legend
7.101	Blue boundary line	Boundary of the Scheme.
7.102	Alternative dash-dot, in blue	Municipal Boundary
7.103	Black line	Planning Unit Boundary
7.104	Area defined by purple line	Detail of the Old City between the walls at a scale of 1:2,500
7.105	Non-coloured area	Area of the Temple Mount and the Western Wall enclave
		Area for detailed planning
7.106	Areas coloured yellow with vertical dark red strips	
7.107	Non-coloured area with black dots	Area for planning after archaeological excavations
7.108	Areas delineated with broken red line	Areas for special architectural treatment
7.109	Areas with vertical purple lines	Areas for restoration and preservation
7.110	Areas with diagonal black lines	Areas reserved for archaeological excavations
7.111	Areas coloured dark yellow	Special residential area
7.112	Areas coloured pink	Residential area No. 1
7.113	Areas coloured yellow	Residential area No. 4
7.114	Areas coloured ochre	Residential area No. 5
7.115	Areas coloured orange	Residential area No. 6
7.116	Areas coloured yellow with vertical vermilion strips and bounded by a dark brown line	Areas for hotels, recreation, institutions and housing
7.117	Areas coloured yellow with vertical vermilion strips and bounded by a red line	Areas for hotels, commerce, institutions and housing
7.118	Areas coloured brown and bounded by a dark brown line	Areas for public buildings
7.119	Areas coloured grey	Commercial area
7.120	Purple line	Commercial frontage
7.121	Areas coloured green	Public open space
7.122	Areas coloured green with vertical strips of dark pink	Public open space for detailed planning
7.123	Areas coloured green and bounded with dark green line	Private open space, for religious buildings and sports activities only
7.124	Areas coloured yellow with green crossed diagonal lines and bounded with a broken dark green line	Declared a cemetery
7.125	Areas coloured with green crossed diagonal lines	Proposed cemetery
7.126	Areas coloured and bounded with dark brown line	Sports area
7.127	Dark red line	Proposed main road
7.128	Light red line	Proposed secondary road
7.129	Circle divided into four parts (upper, lower, right and left), appearing on indicated road:	
	No. in the upper quarter	Road number
	Red number in the right and left quarters	Minimum building line
	Red number in the lower quarter	Road width
7.130	Areas defined by alternative dot-dash, black line	Underground parking

7.2 Zones – Uses of Land and Buildings

7.201 *The area of the Old City*
7.201.1 The area within the Old City is designated for restoration and preservation according to detailed plans, and related to paragraph 7.206 of these regulations.

7.202 *The area of the Temple Mount and the Western Wall Enclave*
7.202.1 On the area of the Temple Mount and the Western Wall enclave, all the restrictions applying to the Old City are to be enforced in accordance with objects of the plan as expressed in paragraph 6.5 of these regulations.
7.202.2 The general character and the buildings of the Temple Mount are to be specially preserved, and no changes will be

allowed to this area except under exceptional circumstances and with the approval of the Local Commission and District Commission.

7.202.3 The Western Wall enclave will be planned as a special area, details of which are to be approved by the relevant committees, in as much as the area is defined as a Holy Place for prayer.

7.203 *Area for Detailed Planning*

7.203.1 These areas are designated for tourist facilities, transport and parking, entertainment, commerce, offices, institutions, civic centres, special housing and public open space. The transport and parking facilities will have to serve the relevant areas and the demands of the Old City between the walls, as to be determined in the detailed plan.

7.204 *Area for Planning after Archaeological Excavations*

7.204.1 The area is to be planned only after the execution and completion of archaeological excavations. The determination of the proposed uses and the detailed plans will require the approval of the Local and District Commissions, co-ordinated with the Director of Antiquities.

7.205 *Area for Special Architectural Treatment*

7.205.1 The area indicated for special architectural treatment is designated for detailed architectural planning.

7.205.2 No land or building in this area is to be used except as indicated in the detailed plan.

7.206 *Area for Restoration and Preservation*

7.206.1 All new buildings, or additions, or the removal of buildings in this area are to be executed with special regard for the particular character of the area. Any development in this area is to be carried out only and exclusively according to detailed plans for restoration and preservation.

7.207 *Special Residential Area 1, 4, 5, 6*

7.207.1 Residential buildings

7.207.2 Residential buildings on two plots with a common wall are subject to approval by the Local Commission and the agreement of the District Commission.

7.207.3 Sports and play grounds, etc., on building sites suited for this purpose, with the approval of the competent building commissions.

7.207.4 Public, religious and educational buildings, museums and schools, on condition that their location and planning are approved by the Local Commission with the agreement of the District Commission.

7.207.5 Offices for members of the free professions and artists.

7.207.6 Convalescence homes and guest-houses.

7.207.7 Shops, on conditions that their uses are as defined in the appendix to the regulations of Outline Plan No. 62

7.208 *Areas for Institutions and Public Buildings*

7.208.1 Buildings associated with institutions including housing and services for the students and staff of the institutions are to be permitted, according to detailed plans and with the approval of the Local Commission and District Commission.

7.208.2 Within the Old City Walls, areas indicated for institutions can include housing.

7.209 *Areas for Hotels, Recreation and Institutions*

7.209.1 In these areas, buildings associated with hotels, recreation and institutions are to be permitted as determined by the detailed plan.

7.210 *Areas for Hotels, Commerce and Institutions*

7.210.1 In these areas, buildings associated with hotels, commerce and institutions and housing as determined by the detailed plan.

7.211 *Areas for Public Buildings*

7.211.1 Public buildings

7.211.2 Places of worship

7.211.3 Cultural and educational centres

7.211.4 Museums and exhibition areas

7.212 *Commercial Areas*

7.212.1 Uses as in residential areas Nos. 1, 4, 5, 6, on condition that residential uses on the ground floor will not be permitted, except with the express approval of the Local Commission and District Commission.

7.212.2 Offices

7.212.3 Shops, workshops; light industrial activities on condition that the uses are in accordance with the attached appendix to Outline Plan No. 62.

7.213 *Commercial Frontage*

7.213.1 In areas where a commercial frontage is indicated, the designation of commercial activities to the road elevation will be permitted even if the area is designated for other uses.

7.213.2 The design of the commercial frontage is to be determined in the detailed plan.

7.214 *Public Open Space*

7.214.1 Public gardens

7.214.2 Sport and games areas except on the public open spaces bordering the Western Wall square on the west.

7.214.3 Buildings ancillary to the above uses with the approval of the Local and District Commissions.

7.214.4 The alignment of roads through public open space is permitted with the approval of the Local and District Commissions.

7.215 *Private Open Space*

7.215.1 As for paragraphs 8.214.1. and 8.214.2.

7.215.2 Places of worship, public educational buildings and ancillary activities which were in existence at the time of approval of this scheme.

7.216 *Declared Cemeteries*

A declared cemetery will be considered as special public space and only the following uses are to be permitted:

7.216.1 Monuments

7.216.2 Associated buildings

The above uses require the approval of the Local Commission and sanction of the District Commission.

7.217 *Proposed Cemetery*

7.217.1 Cemetery

7.217.2 Monuments

7.217.3 Ancillary buildings for the uses in sub-paragraph 1 and 2, with the approval of the Local Commission and the agreement of the District Commission.

7.218 *Sports, Leisure and Recreational Area*

7.218.1 Sports, leisure and recreational facilities.

7.28.2 Sports, leisure and recreational buildings, and ancillary structures — all according to detailed plans.

7.219 *Main Roads and Secondary Roads*

7.219.1 Roads will be detailed within detailed plans.

7.219.2 All road plans, main or secondary, within the area of this scheme must be accompanied by an architectural and landscape treatment plan, in addition to engineering details.

7.220 *Underground Parking*

7.220.1 Any zoning of underground parking necessitates archaeological investigation. Limits of the area will finally be determined only after the completion of archaeological excavations within a detailed plan with the approval of the Local and District Commission and the Director of Antiquities.

8 Restrictions for Ensuring the Control of the Special Architectural Character of the Scheme

8.01 The Requirement for Building in Stone

8.01.1 The external walls of the buildings within the boundary of the scheme (including out-houses, walls and retaining walls) are to be built in natural cut-stone of the type found within each specific area.

8.01.2 The use will not be permitted of any material foreign in character to stone on the external walls, e.g. metal sheeting, concrete or other blocks, in-situ concrete, plaster works, wood or asbestos sheets, except with the approval of the Local Commission and District Commission.

8.02 Building Restrictions near the Old City Walls

8.02.1 Within the Old City, no building is to be erected for any use within 10 metres from the internal face of the wall.

8.02.2 Within the Old City at a distance of up to 50 metres from the internal face of the wall, no building or extension is to be erected for any purpose whatsoever, at an absolute height greater than the wall, and that considered to the nearest point to the building concerned.

8.02.3 Outside the Old City, no building is to be erected, for any purpose whatsoever, within a distance of 75 metres from the outer face of the wall.

8.02.4 Outside the Old City, at a distance of 75 metres from the outer face of the wall, no building or extension is to be erected for any purpose whatsoever, at an absolute height greater than the wall, and that considered to the nearest point to the building concerned. Any deviation from these dimensions requires the approval of the District Commission.

8.02.5 Outside the Old City, at a distance greater than 75 metres as measured from the outer face of the wall, no building or extension is to be erected for any purpose whatsoever, whose absolute height is greater than the absolute height of the wall at a point measured closest to the building concerned multiplied by the factor of the minimum distance of the commencement of building, (i.e. 75 metres) and the total distance between the wall and the building concerned. (Example: If the building in question is situated 150 metres from the outer face of the wall, its height will be $\frac{150}{75} = 2$ times the height of the wall). This restriction applies up to a distance of 150 metres from the outer face of the wall. Any deviation within this paragraph requires the approval of the Local Commission and District Commission.

8.03 The Control of Advertisements, Hoardings and Other Types

8.03.1 The Local Commission is empowered to restrict the form of hoardings and other types of advertisements.

8.03.2 The erection of a sign or its attachment or other forms of advertisement on walls or roofs of houses requires the permission of the Local Commission.

8.04 The Laying of New Telephone Lines

8.04.1 Telephone wires or cables between poles are not to be erected within the area of the scheme.

8.04.2 The telephone system is to be laid underground, and the links to the individual houses are to be executed in accordance with plans approved by the Local Commission.

8.05 Control of Radio and Television Aerials

8.05.1 The Local Commission is empowered to control radio and television aerials; the method and place of their attachment and to demand central collective aerials.

8.06 Control of Sun-heaters

8.06.1 Sun-heaters and ancillary piping which are visible are to be permitted, only with the approval of the Local Commission.

8.07 Electricity Supply and Street Lighting

8.07.1 A building permit for any new work or extension will not be given if the horizontal distance from electricity wires carrying power of 6.3 kilowatts or 22 kilowatt is less than 3 metres, and 2 metres where the power is of low tension.

8.07.2 The erection of poles of steel or wood for carrying electricity wire is to be reduced to a minimum within the boundary of the scheme, and they are to be exchanged for underground cables or wires attached to the walls of buildings in a manner which will not detract from the architectural form of the building and according to a detailed plan.

8.07.3 The Local Commission is empowered to choose special types of street lighting and columns.

8.08 Demolition of Buildings

8.08.1 A permit for the demolition of any building or part of a building will only be given when the following conditions are fulfilled:

8.08.101. The demolition of the building is a consequence of its being unstable and of the City Engineer determining that there is no efficient way of supporting it.

8.08.102 That the demolition of the building or part thereof is necessitated for a road or road widening, or the creation of a public piazza according to an approval detailed plan for the relevant area.

8.08.103 That the demolition of the building be executed according to a detailed plan or an approved Restoration Plan in which a new building follows faithfully the detailed plan as approved by the Local Commission and District Commission.

8.08.104 That the demolition of the building is necessary for the uncovering, or the access to, historic monuments of importance, and is executed with the approval of the Local Commission and District Commission.

8.08.2 A request for a permit for the demolition of a building or part thereof is to be submitted to the Local Commission accompanied by detailed plans of the building to be destroyed, which include measurements, photographs, elevations and stone details of the building to be demolished.

8.08.3 The Local Commission can demand as it sees fit, that the person demolishing a building according to the above permit keep the characteristic building materials, as stone details, stairs, arches, parapets or columns, and reuse these elements in the new building replacing that demolished.

8.09 Planting and the Protection of Existing Growth

8.09.1 Within the boundary of the scheme, no tree shall be uprooted except with the approval of the Local Commission.

8.09.2 The Local Commission is empowered to order landowners to take any action which it sees fit for the protection of any tree on his property or to demand the planting of new trees or other vegetation.

8.10 Sewerage

8.10.1 Any building or extension to a building to be built or restored within the area of this scheme is to be equipped with a sanitary system for sewage disposal, which is to be linked to the Municipal sewage system.

8.10.2 In the planning and execution of sewage works, all steps are to be taken for minimising the damage to ancient buildings above and below ground level, and this with the approval of the Local Commission, the Ministry of Health and the Director of Antiquities.

8.10.3 The installation of a new sewage system or changes within the existing system requires the prior approval of the Local Commission and the Ministry of Health.

Note: Following discussions held by our various planning and building committees, it is contemplated that changes in regulations will be made according to the general principle of restriction and reduction of building and expansion of public open spaces, in order to maintain and enhance the ambiance of the City.

Bazaars and Piazzas

Planning Team for the Old City and its Environs
Arieh Sharon, David Anatol Brutzkus, Eldar Sharon

Jerusalem has always been a centre of commerce for its own population, for the surrounding region and for pilgrims and traders from afar. The Old City retained its flourishing commerce even after a new city began to develop outside its ramparts. At present there are about 1,000 stores in the Old City, apart from numerous workshops and stalls. The oldest commercial streets and bazaars are centrally located along axes laid out in Roman times, although the buildings themselves date back at most to the crusader period. Commerce also developed round the northern and western gates, where buildings were more affected by external influences that changed with the times than those deep inside the city. The unique style and beauty of their architecture make the streets and bazaars of the Old City particularly attractive, and these features should be preserved by skilful renovation and restoration. The changes made in commercial neighbourhoods over the past few decades have tended more and more towards modernisation, thus marring their special character of antiquity. It is therefore necessary to remove all unsuitable additions and restore those sections that have been destroyed.

This proposal presents some examples of how these ancient structures may be adapted to the requirements of modern commerce, while retaining their special charm, such as the installation of appropriate doors, shutters and awnings in stores and canopies shading the streets as protection against sun and rain. These, of course, would involve only changes in architectural detail, but it will be necessary to undertake far more extensive development work in the central commercial areas to achieve architectural harmony.

The central bazaars belong both to the Christian and Moslem Quarters. They are covered alleys, with light and air filtering in through skylights and lateral vents. They are thus cool and shady in summer and sheltered from the wind and rain in winter, so that trade can proceed without interruption at all times of the day and in all seasons. The structures, however, are in a poor state of repair. On the main streets, where commercial premises are in high demand, every nook and cranny is converted into a store by the judicious (but ugly) use of a few tin sheets. This obviously disfigures the ancient buildings and, moreover, mars the view. Many stalls were attached to buildings and in the course of time have been converted into semi-permanent structures put together from old pieces of wood and tin. While in the main streets a great effort is made to decorate the stores — however deplorable the type of decoration may be — the stores in the more remote areas are very poorly maintained. Over the years many of the buildings have been divided up among different tenants, and commercial fronts are often split up and disturb the original structure. In those parts where there is a lively tourist traffic, tradesmen seek to attract business by the display of ostentatious signs, posters and pseudo-modern trappings.

Moreover, the preset store-shutters, casement-shutters and awnings are unsightly and out of keeping with the ancient architecture. The entire bazaar area is sorely in need of cleaning and renovation.

To preserve the characteristic appearance of the Old City streets, it is therefore essential:
1   To enforce strict compliance with the Jerusalem by—law requiring that all buildings be made of stone.
2   To provide for proper signs and posters.
3   To determine the appropriate architectural design for the type of awning or shutters to be used, in harmony with the original style of the buildings.

As an example of how this may be effected we offer some detailed suggestions of awnings, shutters or canopies (see drawings).

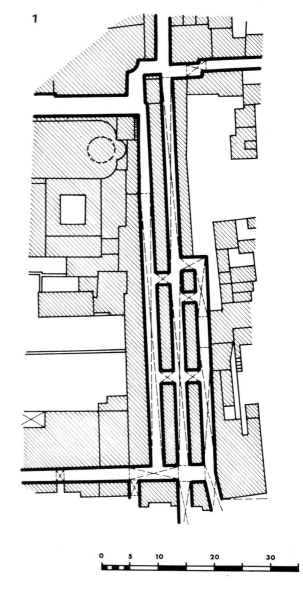

1

1   Plan of central bazaars
2   The arched roof of the bazaar
3   Detail from the Goldsmiths' Bazaar
4   The central bazaar

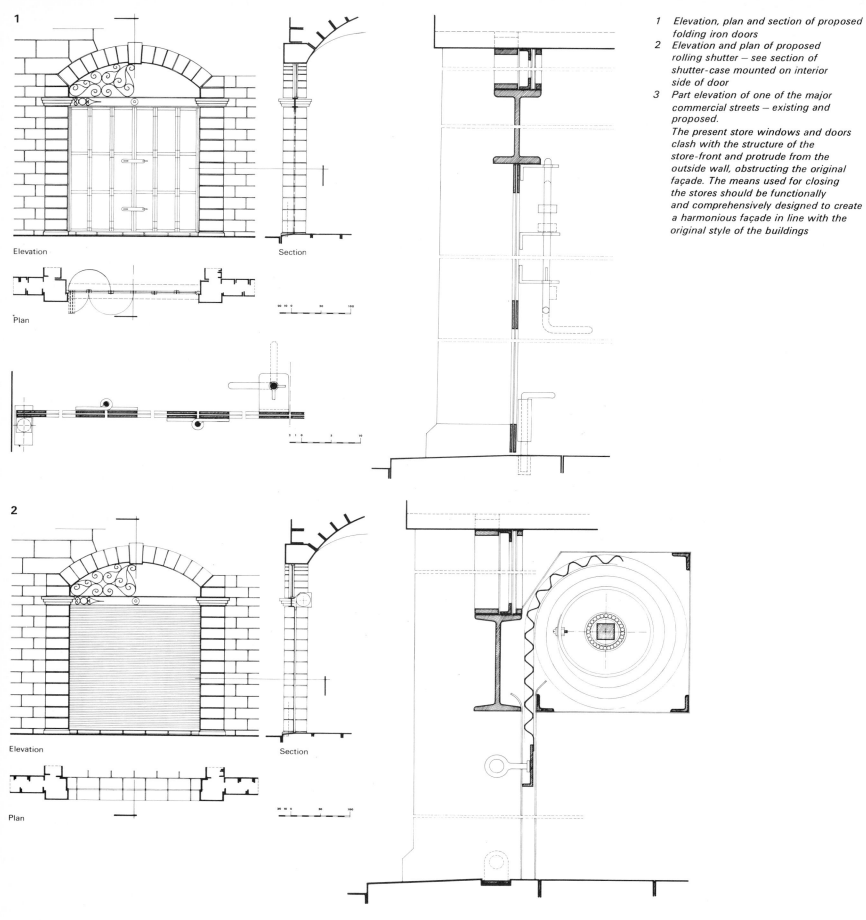

1 Elevation, plan and section of proposed folding iron doors

2 Elevation and plan of proposed rolling shutter — see section of shutter-case mounted on interior side of door

3 Part elevation of one of the major commercial streets — existing and proposed.
The present store windows and doors clash with the structure of the store-front and protrude from the outside wall, obstructing the original façade. The means used for closing the stores should be functionally and comprehensively designed to create a harmonious façade in line with the original style of the buildings

Elevation

Section

Plan

Elevation

Section

Plan

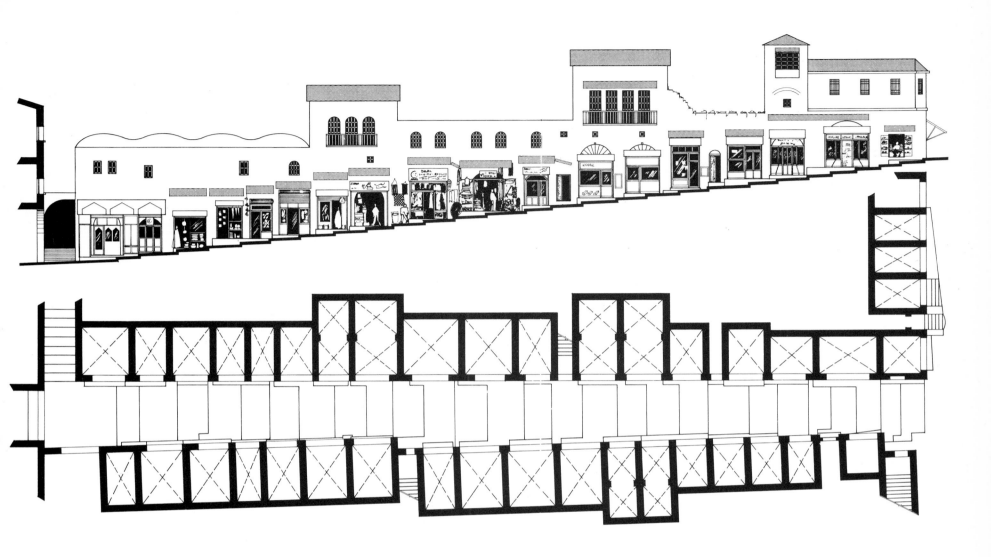

Proposed renovation of store-fronts on David Street

Jaffa Gate

The plans call for the restoration of the grandeur of the spacious piazza inside Jaffa Gate, dominated by the impressive northern section of the Citadel. The unsightly awnings and other additions which hide the original structures opposite the Citadel should be removed and the original façades brought back into view by clearance or restoration.

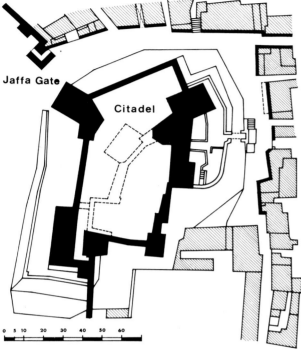

Jaffa Gate

Citadel

0 5 10   20   30   40   50   60

1

2

1 Plan of Jaffa Gate. In the centre, the Citadel with its square surrounded by store-fronts
2 View of the interior piazza, the main entrance to the Old City from western Jerusalem and a major tourist and commercial axis
3 View from Jaffa Gate onto the entrance to the bazaar area

3

Damascus Gate

The Damascus Gate, surpassing all the other gates in beauty and splendour, was, in earlier times, as impressive from the inside as it was from the outside. Today there is little evidence of the glorious piazza onto which visitors once emerged upon entering the gate. It is now cluttered with unsightly stores and stalls spread haphazardly over the broad paving stones, burying the beauty of the gate's inner façade. The plans call for the restoration and site improvement of this spacious square by the removal of all stalls and the relocation of the stores on the western side of the piazza. It is also recommended that the ancient Roman city gate, which lies below the existing level, should be re-opened, thereby giving access to the renovated ancient square, which would be appropriately connected with the upper piazza.

1

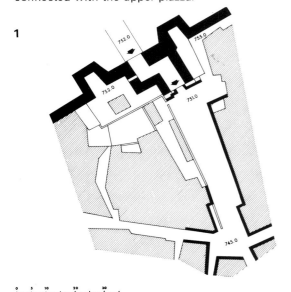

2

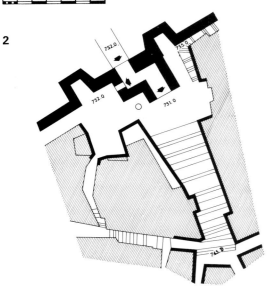

1   *Plan of existing inner square of the Gate*
2   *Proposal for a more spacious interior piazza*
3   *Inner façade of the Gate, with steps descending to the bazaars*

3

169

Herod's Gate

The original narrow side entrance to Herod's Gate, which links the residential area of the Moslem Quarter with the commercial area outside the walls, was closed at the end of the last century and replaced by a wider frontal opening. The chambers of the gate itself and the small square inside the city into which it opens are now crowded with numerous stalls that disfigure the area, obstruct the view and interfere with pedestrian movement. The plans call for clearing the original open space inside the gate by removing the stalls in the small square and the private vegetable plots adjoining the eastern edge of the gate, thereby restoring the full beauty of the steps and the inner façade of gate and walls. It is also recommended that the original side entrance be re-opened. Under this proposal, gate and piazza would provide a fitting entrance to the Moslem Quarter.

Planning proposals are therefore presented for the bazaars, the façades of the stores and for the inside of the main gates.

Steps leading from Herod's Gate to the Moslem Quarter

1 Plan showing existing situation inside
 the Gate (see photographs below)
2 Proposal for a more spacious interior
 piazza
3 Inner façade of the Gate; with steps
 descending to the bazaars.

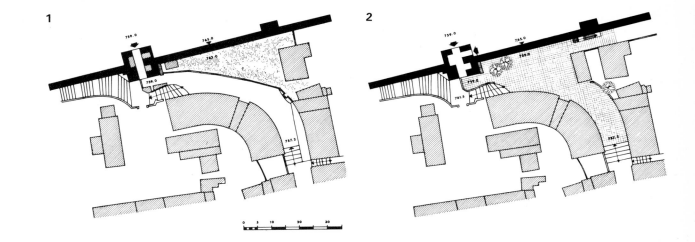

1

Restoration of the Pool of Hezekiah

Planning Team for the Old City and its Environs
Arieh Sharon, David Anatol Brutzkus, Eldar Sharon
Ass. Architect: Shlomo Khayat.

This pool, reached through Jaffa Gate and
just north of David Street, has been in existence
since the period of the Second Temple, when it was
called the Pool of the Towers (the towers of
Herod's Palace, the site of the present Citadel,
stood nearby). In crusader times it was called
the Pool of the Baths, for its waters fed the
ancient baths to the east. It was connected with
the Mamilla Pool (which is outside the walls) by
a subterranean canal which was blocked during the
War of Independence. The Pool of Hezekiah is now
surrounded by dwellings and almost inaccessible.
It is dry, abandoned and neglected. It is therefore
proposed to restore the pool and once again fill it
with water; build a promenade around it; provide
adequate access to it; develop a new commercial
front in the existing buildings along the new
promenade; and restore the Coptic khan overlooking
the pool.

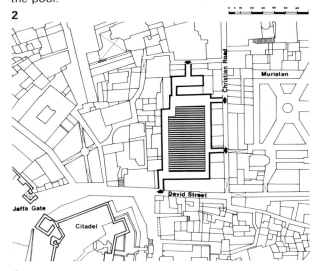

1 Part of the old buildings rising above
   the pool
2 Plan of Hezekiah's Pool with proposed
   approaches from the bazaars and the
   Christian Quarter
3 A 19th-century photograph of Hezekiah's
   Pool showing water level
4 The eastern façade of the pool

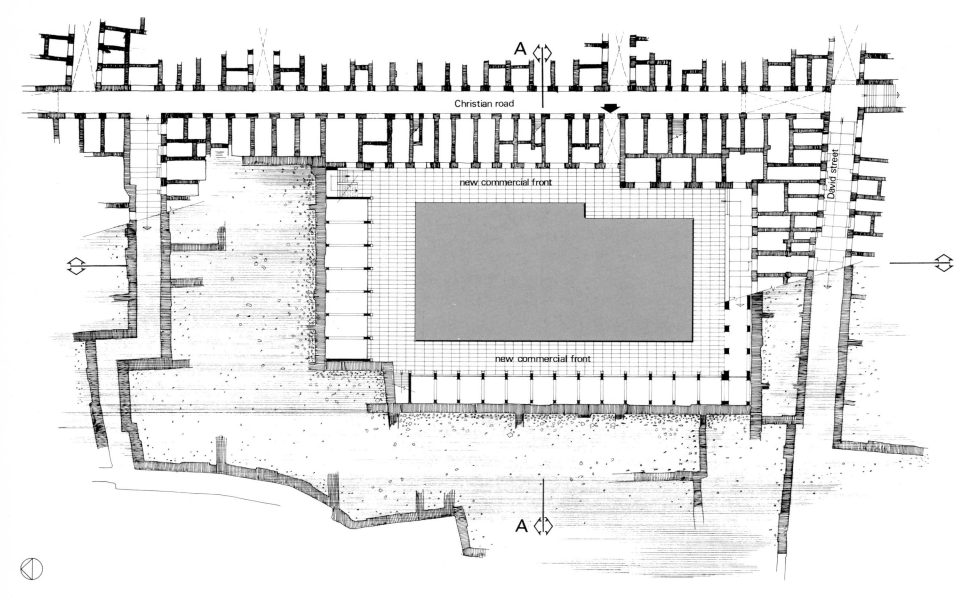

Christian road

A

new commercial front

new commercial front

David street

A

East-west section A-A

Proposed plan for restoration of Hezekiah's Pool. Water level and the Christian Road

opposite *Proposed upper level with existing plan for Citadel piazza and Coptic khan*

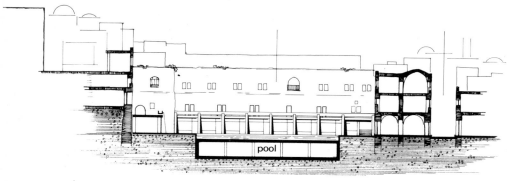

pool

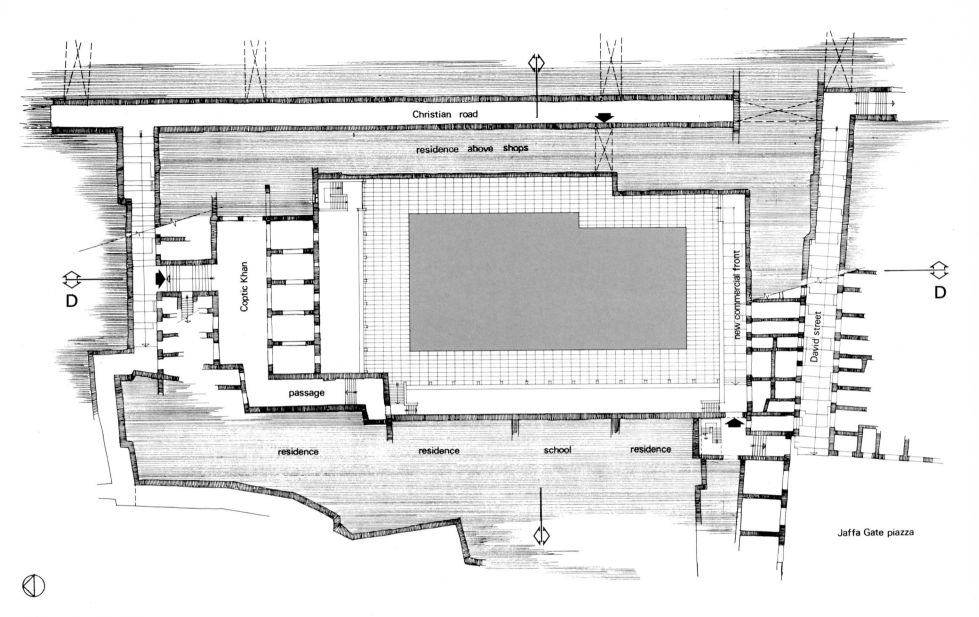

Christian road

residence above shops

Coptic Khan

new commercial front

David street

passage

D

D

residence   residence   school   residence

Jaffa Gate piazza

North-south section D-D

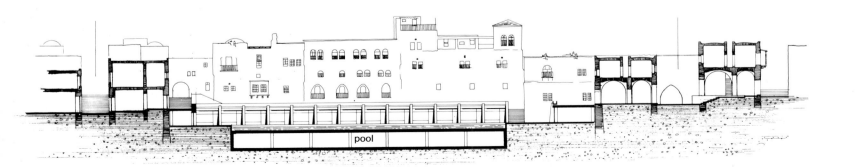

pool

175

Buildings in the Jewish Quarter. In the
foreground a fully restored dome; in the
background buildings awaiting
restoration

Reconstruction of the Jewish Quarter

Planning Team of the Company for Reconstruction
and Development in the Jewish Quarter in the
Old City.
Director General: M. Avnieli
Architect in charge: S. Gardi

Jewish resettlement in what had once been the
all-Jewish city of Jerusalem was concentrated
throughout the centuries in what subsequently
became known as the Jewish Quarter. From the
thirteenth century on, this area extended from the
eastern slopes of Mount Zion to the remains of the
Western Wall on the Temple Compound. The size of
the Quarter has changed from generation to
generation, and so has its population, which was
at its largest half-way through the nineteenth
century, when 15,000 Jews lived there out of a
total Old City population of 28,000. Overcrowding
was a feature of the entire city.

The events of 1920 and 1929 and the rapid
development of the new city of Jerusalem outside
the walls of the Old City brought about a decline
in its population. On the eve of the War of
Independence there were only 5,100 people in the
Jewish Quarter. In May 1948 they were overcome
after months of siege and battle, and the survivors
were either taken prisoner or evacuated to the new
city. The Jewish Quarter was largely destroyed or
ruined. The Six Day War of June 1967 restored the
Quarter to the Jews. At that time it was inhabited by
almost 5,000 poverty-stricken Arabs, most of them
refugees living in primitive conditions, with an
average of four people to a room.

The Israeli Government decided to resettle and
reconstruct the Jewish Quarter as soon as possible.
For this purpose, a special committee was set up
under the direct authority of the Prime Minister.
It embarked on the task of gathering information
and carrying out physical, demographic, historic
and archaeological surveys. The borders of the new
quarter were determined on the basis of data received
from these studies. Its size differed little from that
of the Jewish Quarter over the past century. The
borders were, in the east, the Western Wall; in the
south, the city wall; in the west, the Armenian
Monastery and its complex of buildings; and in the
north, Shalshelet Street, one of the important
streets in the Old City. The area measures about

140 dunams (35 acres) and comprises 16 per cent
of the total area of the Old City. Out of this area
55 per cent is built-up, and the other 45 per cent
is partly or totally destroyed.
A government authority, the Company for
Reconstruction and Development in the Jewish
Quarter in the Old City, was placed in charge of its
development. The company is run and financed by
the government. Its aim is to develop the Jewish
Quarter as a national, religious and historic site,
which includes a residential area and public
services for its inhabitants and visitors.

The company's first move was to prepare a
masterplan in line with the surveys which had
been carried out. The purpose of the plan was to
direct the process of development and construction.
Furthermore, the company renovated buildings and
cleared ruins, so as to restore *yeshivot* which had
existed in the Quarter for many centuries before
its capture.

The Jewish Quarter was always a residential area
which consisted of many synagogues, *yeshivot*,
Jewish religious seminaries and a commercial centre.
Only a part of the houses, shops and a few
synagogues have remained, and those to be found
today are either being renovated, such as the four
Sepharadi synagogues (see project page 184),
Haramban and Hakaraim, or being newly planned,
such as the Hurvah and Nissan Beck. Some of the
yeshivot have already been re-established (Porat
Yoseph and Etz Haim). The commercial centre will
be reconstructed as part of the central bazaar area,
which is so prominent in the Old City. Steps have
been constructed along the descent to the Western
Wall, forming part of the central horizontal axis
leading from the bazaar area to the Western Wall
piazza. An underground terminal is now planned for
parking and various other services which will be
linked to the commercial centre. This will be located
in the southern sector of the city, close to the south
wall, and the entrance will be under the south wall
via a circular road. Residential quarters and hotels

will be built above the parking lot.

It is the intention to preserve the residential
character of the Jewish Quarter, which should
eventually house 600–700 families and 1000 to 1,500
yeshiva students, making a total of 4,500 to 5,000
people. The plan also calls for 200–250 stores and
two or three hotels.

The Jewish Quarter is an integral part of the
Old City. Most of its buildings are one to two hundred
years old, with parts dating back even further. Apart
from a few synagogues, which are much older,
it has hardly any historical monuments, but it does
excel in close stonework, narrow lanes, inner
courtyards, arched spaces and domes, which are
worth preserving. It is to this end that reconstruction
is carried out in keeping with the existing style.
The work includes renovation of existing buildings,
the completion of partially ruined buildings and
complete reconstruction of destroyed and evacuated
areas. The building material used is rectangular
natural stone, processed by hand and placed one on
top of the other. The buildings are two to four storeys
high, so as not to spoil the skyline, and most of
them have inner courtyards. The lanes, 2.5 to 4
metres wide, are to be used only by pedestrians.
The shops and houses will be serviced by special
vehicles suited to negotiate the lanes. Close
attention was given to the replanning of alleyways
and squares. Pavement stones, lighting sources,
benches and the like are being designed and built
by the company. To supplement the present poor
service infrastructure (a holdover from Turkish
rule), a new underground infrastructure network
has been planned and is being implemented.
The combination of old and new expresses
itself not only in the style of the buildings
but also in the structure of the Quarter.
The system of lanes is mainly based on that prior
to 1948, with certain changes and slight additions,
particularly in the centre of the Quarter and in
the new approaches to the Western Wall that have
been planned and are being built.

Western Wall Area

Dung Gate

Zion Gate

0 20 40 60 80 100 m.

The company's planning team, which was set up specifically for this purpose, carried out the surveys and prepared the masterplan. The detailed schemes, including the renovations, were done simultaneously by the planning team and different groups of private architects.

To date, 10,000 square metres of public buildings and forty residential units have been renovated. About 350 young people, in the framework of *yeshivot* and Fighting Pioneering Youth (Nahal), and about forty-five young couples live in the Quarter today.

There is a continuous flow of visitors, tourists and worshippers to the Western Wall, and this ensures constant movement through the Jewish Quarter. This stream of people, on the one hand, and the permanent population, on the other, together with the public institutions and the shops, all ensure a flourishing and lively Jewish Quarter.

Jewish Quarter – Masterplan

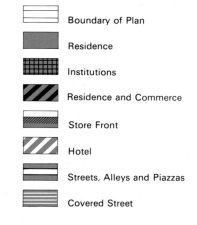

Boundary of Plan

Residence

Institutions

Residence and Commerce

Store Front

Hotel

Streets, Alleys and Piazzas

Covered Street

178

Problems and Architectural Guide-Lines in Restoration and Reconstruction

The regulations of the detailed scheme determined the planning principles, which are in force in the Jewish Quarter today:

1   Only *stone* will be used in building construction. A regulation to this effect applies to all of Jerusalem and in the case of the Jewish Quarter it will be strictly enforced. There is a sharp conflict between the traditional building techniques in the Old City and those available today. The problem is not only financial, but mostly technical — the ability to do the work the available know-how and the influence of the techniques and culture of the twentieth century. The use of modern techniques (such as prefabricated elements) was often considered but rejected for several reasons, the principal one being the difficulties in using cranes and derricks in the narrow alleyways of the Quarter.

2   The *height* of new dwelling units is not to exceed two to four floors, in line with the existing tradition and so as to conform with the surrounding townscape.

3   *Vehicular traffic* within the Quarter will be forbidden. Movement in the Quarter will be restricted to *pedestrians.* The complex of routes basically corresponds with historic passageways in the Jewish Quarter, so as to retain the link with the past and with the special character of the Quarter and its alleys. For special duty services, such as garbage collection, fire extinction, ambulances and transportation of goods, a system of electrically powered vehicles, easily manoeuvrable in the narrow lanes, is being considered and planned.

4   The *preservation* of existing domes and arched structures and especially façades which are of architectonic value is to be strictly observed.

5   *Infrastructure* of utility services. A widescale plan was drawn up for various utility services, including drainage and sewerage lines, water pipes, telephone lines and electrical cables, all to be installed underground.

6   All *street surfacing* in the Old City is to follow the original stone-paving pattern. The problem of *covering the streets,* to enable pedestrians to move freely even in extreme climatic conditions, has been the subject of several surveys. Different kinds of awnings have been proposed (see project on page 162). The complex of alleyways itself has been studied in relation to the problems of drainage and sewerage. In many places the surface level of the alleys was lowered by as much as two metres below the original level.

7   *Layout of new dwellings.* The principles of design and planning of housing which have governed building in the Old City for

Development of Batei Machase Piazza

Architect: Saadia Mandl

generations are being applied in the present reconstructions. The height of the blocks of buildings, the inner complex of passageways and the shared courtyards were all planned according to traditional layouts. Cross-sections of the area and different views were all carefully studied. Each detailed plan is checked after a model of the blocks and of the surroundings has been completed. Generally, the buildings border the street, while their façades overlook an internal courtyard which serves as the entrance to a number of housing units. The progression from private to public space is achieved in a number of steps: the private house, the common courtyard, the passageway shared by a number of courtyards leading to an alley or to the public square. Wherever possible, this ancient pattern of building has been retained in reconstruction of new housing units, and entire building blocks, bordered by alleys and interspersed by patios and piazzas, were treated as architectural ensembles.

1 South façade of Rothschild House and Beit Hasofer as they were found in June 1967 before reconstruction
2 Proposition for the reconstruction of Batei Machase Piazza
3 Rothschild House before reconstruction
4 South-eastern view of the largely reconstructed piazza

3

4

Ground-level plan. Note the thoroughfare to the Western Wall shaded dark, open spaces and piazzas light grey

Restoration of the Sephardi Synagogues

Sponsored by The Jerusalem Foundation
Architect in charge: Dan Tanai

The four adjoining Sepharadi synagogues, Eliyahu Hanavi, Istanbuli, Yohanan Ben Zakkai and the Emtzai, are all to be found on one site east of the Jewish Quarter Road in the Old City. They have several features in common: their floors are at least 3 metres lower than the surrounding street level, and their roofs do not protrude in height, but form a continuous whole together with the surrounding roofs; they have no exterior windows, only windows facing the interior courtyards; and their entrances are modestly concealed. These features shed light on the hostile attitude of the non-Jewish inhabitants towards the houses of Jewish worship, which, in turn, conditioned the outward appearance of these synagogues; an agglomeration of buildings, unremarkable from the outside, concealing from the passer-by the spaciousness of their interior.

The construction of the four Sepharadi synagogues began in the sixteenth century — after the destruction of the twelfth-century Nahmanides Synagogue used by Jewish exiles from Spain — and building continued in the centuries that followed. With the fall of the Old City and its occupation by the Jordanians in 1948, the buildings were heavily damaged and their interior totally destroyed. Restoration work began immediately after the Six Day War. The area was cleared and the beauty of the original structures revived.

Two of the synagogues, Yohanan Ben Zakkai and the Emtzai, are both long structures with vaulted roofs. The two other synagogues have four pillars which arch upwards to support a windowed drum topped by a cupola. All four buildings share a noticeable lack of any overall design conception. They simply grew from their original core in a somewhat naive though organic manner, clearly influenced by the traditions and tastes of members of the community who came from various countries. This influence is most marked in the interior of the synagogues.

Among the decorative stonework, the most striking is the western façade of the Emtzai Synagogue. One of the curiosities of this façade is that one of the filigreed fan-lights flanking the door is round, while the other is square. The Spanish influence can be seen in the shape of the windows of Yohanan Ben Zakkai and the Istanbuli, their curved top following the Moorish style of a 'Camel Back'. There is also a trace of the Moorish element in the Gothic front of the Holy Ark in Yohanan Ben Zakkai.

After the Six Day War, all four synagogues, in a state of ruin and decay, were cleared of debris that had piled up to a height of more than 3 meters and were stripped of their plaster, revealing architectural features belonging to different periods of the last four hundred years. In general, it was found that the earlier the period, the more beautiful the design.

With the exception of Yohanan Ben Zakkai, which had a Carrara marble floor, all the floors were tiled in smooth Jerusalem stone. Walls, pillars and arches were all built of various types of this stone, reflecting the different phases of their construction. Special effort and considerable labour went into the restoration of the stone walls, and the beauty of the original facade may now be seen again. Only where the material in the later building was not of stone, such as the vaults and cupolas, was there a need to restore with plaster.

The domes were covered with small Jerusalem-stone tiles in various shades, as are most of the buildings in the Old City. The windows of Eliyahu Hanavi and the Istanbuli were mainly in the base of the drum and beneath the cupola. It is doubtful that at such a height they were ever opened. It was therefore decided to replace them with small stone-framed windows similar to those of twelfth-century Spanish synagogues. Following the ancient method, glass medallions in various shades were used, through which rays of sunlight are filtered across the whole of the interior.

As we have observed, the original entrances were concealed, and the doors were made of simple undecorated wood. The new doors will be of bronze, to be designed by the winners of an artists' contest.

The most sumptuous part of the synagogues before their destruction in 1948 was their furnishings, particularly the dais (almemor) and the Holy Ark. Ancient daises, Holy Arks and candelabras from Italy and Spain have been used in the restoration. They are well suited to the spaciousness of these synagogues and re-create the traditional atmosphere and beauty of Jewish houses of worship in bygone generations.

1

2

3

4

1 18th-century Interior of Eliahu Hanavi
 Synagogue
2 The Central Synagogue after restoration
3 Restored inner façade of Eliahu
 Hanavi Synagogue
4 Restored and partially refurnished
 Yochanan Ben Zakkai Synagogue
 with the Holy Ark in the background

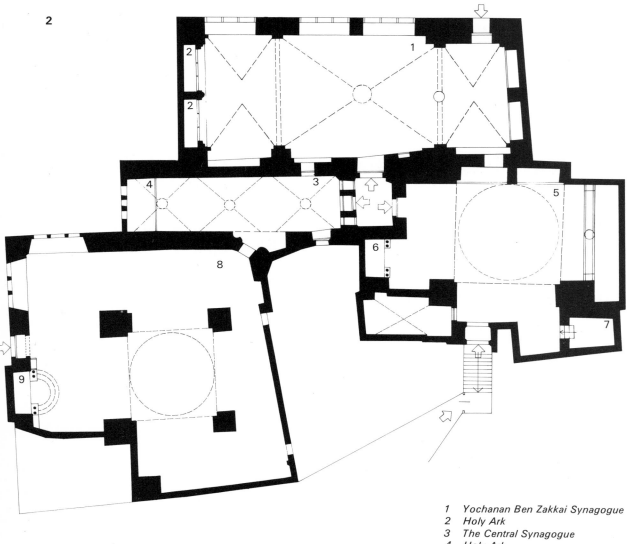

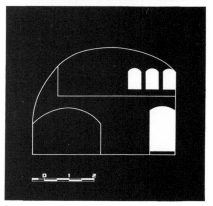

1 North-south section
2 Plan of the four synagogues
3 Schemes of various window patterns
opposite *Interiors prior to restoration,
after removal of debris*

1 Yochanan Ben Zakkai Synagogue
2 Holy Ark
3 The Central Synagogue
4 Holy Ark
5 Eliahu Hanavi Synagogue
6 Holy Ark
7 The Cave
8 Istanbuli Synagogue
9 Holy Ark

Mount Scopus Campus – Masterplan
The Hebrew University of Jerusalem

General Layout Scheme: D. Reznik, S. Shaked
architects, townplanners
Academic Campus Masterplan:
D. Reznik, R. Karmi, H. Katzeff, architects.

After the War of Independence and the creation of the State of Israel in 1948, the Hebrew University campus on Mount Scopus was cut off from West Jerusalem and remained deserted, except for a skeleton maintenance staff, for almost twenty years. During this period the university began its construction programme on the Givat Ram campus in the western part of the city. The Hebrew University, centre of higher education and research in the city of Jerusalem and the State of Israel, once again became a physical entity with its own campus.

The reunification of Jerusalem in 1967 made the rehabilitation and development of the campus on Mount Scopus possible. The reconstruction programme, which began without delay, provided for the transfer from Givat Ram to Mount Scopus of the following faculties: Humanities, Social Sciences, Natural Sciences (first year studies only), Law and the School of Education. Under the completed programme the restored campus will serve a student population of some 13,500. Mount Scopus rises to a height of 825 metres above sea level and overlooks the Judean Desert and the Dead Sea to the east and the city of Jerusalem to the south and west. The university campus covers, on both sides of the ridge, an area of more than 200 acres, most of it on sloped terrain swept by winter rains of considerable intensity and by penetrating north-west winds. The boundaries of the site were finally determined by physical conditions and government planning requirements.

The road network is based on the integration of two complementary patterns. The first pattern is based mainly on the university-controlled road which is to provide access to the campus, both for public transport and service traffic; the second on a peripheral road providing access for private cars. This ring-road feeds large parking areas.

The academic campus has been located on the ridge of Mount Scopus, thus focusing the main activity around the existing buildings with future expansion provided for the steeper slopes to the east, where building operations are more expensive. The students' residences, housing more than 5,000 single students and some 800 families, are to be built simultaneously with the academic campus. These residences are linked to the University Sports Centre and are surrounded by open green areas which are to form part of the National University Park on Mount Scopus.

The design principles emerged from the attempt to utilise the special character of the site in order to satisfy the basic needs of university life in all its ramifications. A university education and an academic society should do more than serve the immediate purpose of the transmission and acquisition of knowledge. They should also encourage the full expression of the individual personality. The aim of the design was therefore to create an environment conducive to the widening of human horizons, befitting an intellectual centre, enabling the student to pursue his studies under ideal conditions, both meeting the teacher's requirements in carrying out individual research and offering the opportunity to merge into an harmonious community. Thus, the masterplan proposes a spatial organisation based on the parallelism of different systems, each built at a different level, but all connected by vertical feeders.

Service – Transport System

The lower level of the campus provides the buildings with services and technical facilities. Ranged along the covered road are the workshops and storage areas, air-raid shelters, air-conditioning and electrical substations, loading and unloading platforms.
Public transport is to be given preference over private cars. Buses will therefore reach the

Panoramic view of Mount Scopus. White line indicates planned skyline of the academic campus

campus directly at the main Student Mall through the university-controlled central road. Parking facilities are provided at the same level, with private cars using the peripheral road network to reach the campus.

Pedestrian System

The teaching spine forms the main pedestrian indoor level, where the various-sized lecture rooms are located (thus concentrating the teaching activities of the campus). Also on this level are the Student Mall, the Shopping Centre, the Akademon Bookstore, the Sculpture Garden and the Synagogue, the main dining halls and some of the cafeterias, which complement the social activities and encourage mixing among the various elements of the total community.

The Outdoor System

The plaza level is the main outdoor spine – the social spine – on which the entrance to every building on the campus is located. It is at this level that every faculty and department is identified by its entrance, by its relation, inwardly, to the

heart of the campus, and outwardly, to the panorama of Jerusalem. Also on this level are the university's central institutions – the Library, the Auditorium and the Faculty Club – each adding its special charm and distinctive grace to the beauty of the campus.

The Teaching System

All upper-building levels are reserved for faculty members' offices, providing teachers with privacy to meet students individually or in small seminars. These faculty offices form a kind of belt surrounding the university pedestrian spine, ensuring economy of services and facilities and the exchange of ideas and equipment. The unbroken continuum of teaching and living spaces forms an integrated architectural and urban landscape, rather than a collection of disparate campus buildings.

Conclusions

Concentration will help the university serve as a centre where activities merge and the individual can sense his identity with the whole.

Limitation of spread will help the university preserve the natural landscape and the existing skyline and ensure the time-scale principle of a pedestrian campus.

Separation of pedestrian and vehicular traffic will allow private, public and service cars to reach their destinations without restricting the free flow of pedestrian movement. Parking can then be contained within the area of building, avoiding a concentration of cars on the adjoining landscape.

Growth system will aid the university in meeting the changing needs of the academic programme. It will provide the university with an overall framework, the nucleus of which is the five-year development plan, and enable each stage to grow organically, without producing an architectural jungle.

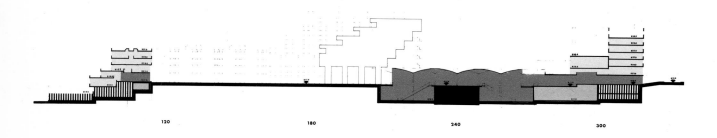

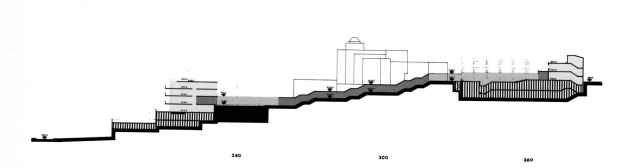

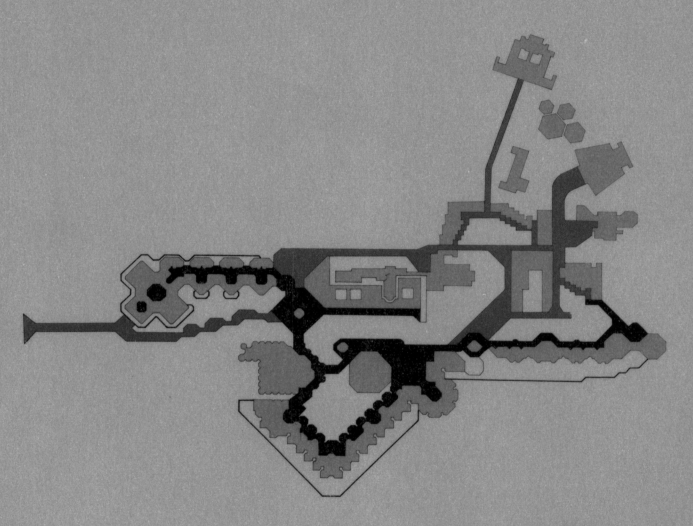

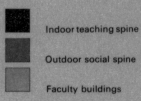

Indoor teaching spine

Outdoor social spine

Faculty buildings

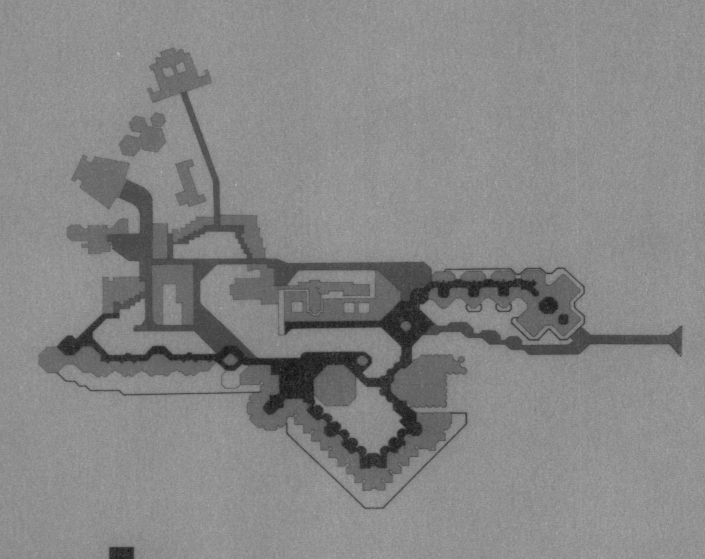

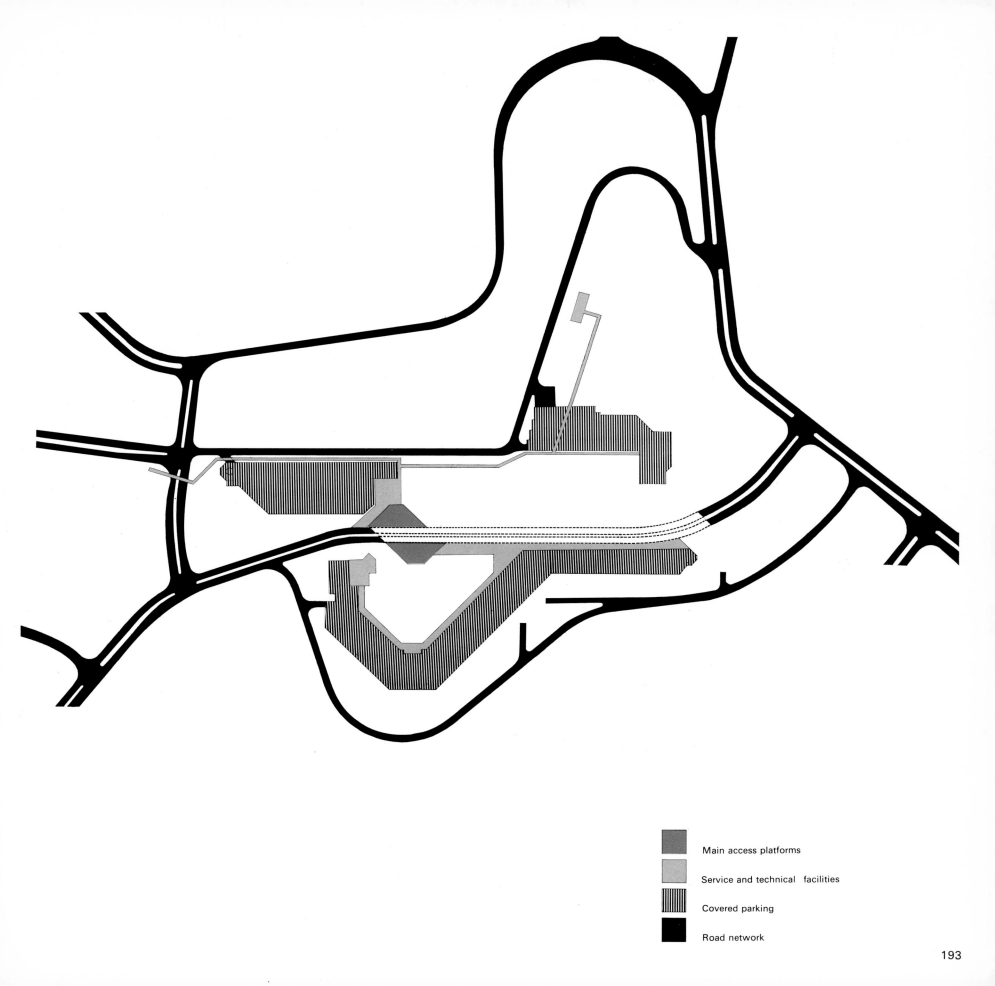

Main access platforms

Service and technical facilities

Covered parking

Road network

193

Zahal Square-Jaffa Gate

Architects: Arieh Sharon, Eldar Sharon

Before the Six Day War, derelict structures, shacks and rubble blocked the view of the west wall, especially in the Jaffa Gate area. The Jerusalem Municipality accordingly decided to clear the entire area so that the whole wall would be restored to view. The stretch of land between the New Gate and Jaffa Gate was levelled and provisionally planted, and, with the newly recovered space from demolition, the former roads leading north and south were widened.

This provisional solution was followed by a decision of the Municipality and the National Parks Authority which called for the preparation of a comprehensive development project. The first phase included the conversion of the empty and neglected patch of land lying in the recessed north-west corner of the city wall into a well-organised, paved garden-piazza — to be named Zahal Square — and the creation of a new and wider approach route for pedestrians leading from this square to Jaffa Gate. In a later phase of the plan, it is proposed to construct an underground car-park near the gate, which all would then enter on foot.

The new promenade, which follows the projections of the west wall, is separated from the existing motor-road by a planted garden strip, which protects the pedestrian from the dust and noise of the traffic. (Under the provisional proposal, the pedestrian path was to be adjacent to the road; it has now been moved close to the wall.)

It is thus seen that there is immediate emphasis in the first phase of the plan — almost completed — on the provision of a gentle, pleasing, pedestrian approach-way to Jaffa Gate from Zahal Square, inducing the appropriate mood of tranquillity and security from passing cars in the visitor about to enter the walled city of Jerusalem. The garden-piazza at Zahal Square, which lies along the visual axis of the existing Jaffa Road and the new promenade, will contribute to this mood, with the modular division of its paving and the clusters of palm trees which it is proposed to plant. The pedestrian will cross the slightly sloped garden-piazza along a diagonal path to meet the beginning of the new promenade and continue along the wall up to Jaffa Gate. As the pedestrian nears the gate, the new National Park which is planned for the Hinnom Valley will come into broad view.

1

1 Original approach to Jaffa Gate from the west
2 Plan for Zahal Square and promenade leading to Jaffa Gate
3 Completed promenade
4 Western perspective of city wall from Zahal Square to Jaffa Gate

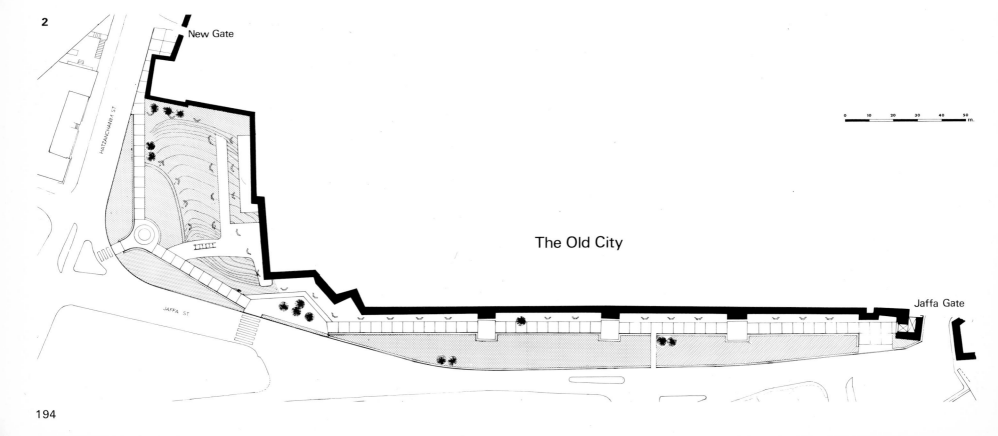

2

New Gate

The Old City

Jaffa Gate

3

4

Jerusalem National Park

Preliminary proposal by the National Parks Authority
Prepared by a National Parks Authority Team,
headed by Arye Dvir, Landscape Architect

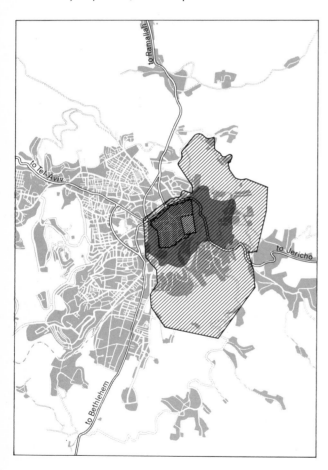

The historic area around the Old City was designated as a National Park. The preliminary masterplan sets out the aims and basic ideas of the proposed park. The first part of the plan has been formally approved and development work has begun. The second part of the plan is expected to be approved shortly.

The proposed area consists of the biblical, now mostly barren, valleys of Hinnom and Kidron; the adjoining hills to the east, south and west; and a narrow strip of built-up land on the north and north-west with a road separating the city wall from the adjacent densely built-up residential quarter. The whole area covers some 2,400 dunams (600 acres) of which 800 dunams are already being developed.

It is an area of unique historic importance and the beauty of its natural landscape has been enriched by a treasury of handsome structures of various periods, monuments to the peoples and cultures of ages past.

The Problems

The continued existence of this unique heritage is, however, not automatically guaranteed. Indeed, it faces grave dangers, not to individual shrines but to the area as an integrated whole, a unity comprising diverse elements in delicate balance. The dangers stem from four main sources:

1   The site is already a powerful focus of attraction for large crowds and will long remain so, yet it is unprepared to cope with mass visits.

2   It is lacking in the basic services and amenities for visitors. This prompts haphazard solutions to the immediate need and may stimulate piecemeal activity with harmful long-term results. Whatever is done should be done only in accordance with a well-conceived masterplan.

3   The structural trend in the twentieth century favours vast size and scale. This is true of both highways and buildings. Such a pattern, however, would be totally wrong in and near the vicinity of the Old City and do untold harm to the historic site. But without a masterplan, individual builders may launch works which later become *faits accomplis*.

4   The capacity of modern technology rapidly to change a country's landscape is often regarded as one of its principal virtues. Jerusalem is one landscape where the major impact of technology may make an impetuous change irrevocable. Imaginative planning must utilise present-day technology to preserve and beautify this site, not to efface, replace or overwhelm.

The Aims

The aims of the National Parks Authority are to seek solutions and safeguards to the aforesaid problems and challenges by:

1   Planning the area as one integral theme, masterminded by a single design team which will coordinate the requirements of all the diverse factors involved and fashion them into one overall plan.

2   Providing and maintaining an appropriate setting for the existing shrines and monuments.

3   Serving as a 'binding' element for the various structures of divergent styles by imaginative landscaping.

4   Creating a green belt, alive with people (with adequate foot-paths and promenades for them) around the city walls, which would form a vibrant unifying element binding the old town with the new.

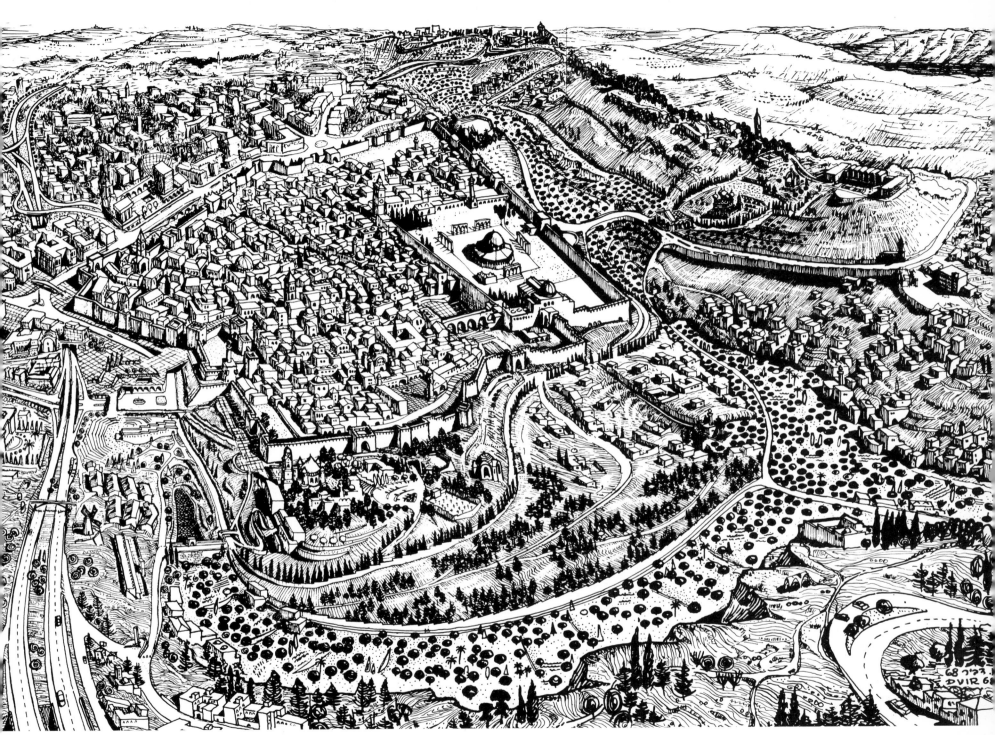

*Perspective of National Park area as seen
from the south
overleaf National Park area
showing, from left to right, Mount
Scopus and the Mount of Olives with
necropolis. In the foreground Absalom's
Pillar, Tomb of the priestly family Hezir
and the Pyramid of Zacharia*

199

The City Walls

1 *Scale.* The city walls should determine the scale of the elements around them: huge retaining walls, large-scale highway construction, as well as high monumental buildings, will compete with and dwarf the walls. These must be avoided — or at least be kept at a safe distance.

2 *Excavation.* Except for a small section in the north, the lowest courses of the walls go down in some cases to a depth of as much as 15 metres beneath the centuries' old accumulation of earth and debris. In certain selected places the debris should be removed so as to expose the full might and grandeur of the walls and bring into view the huge stones of Herod's construction. The moat on the western edge of the Tower of David should be cleared.

3 *Early Wall Sections.* Sections of early walls belonging to the periods of the City of David and the Second Temple have been discovered. They are, however, not discernible to the layman; nor can he follow the development of the wall construction throughout Jerusalem's history. Some should be excavated and partially reconstructed, and the continued courses of these early walls should be clearly marked, particularly at the corners and the gates, with appropriate posts and signs, or even, where possible, by a special track. Such visual aids would be a boon to visitors, enlivening and simplifying the complex archaeological history of the site.

4 *Tours of the Battlements.* Tours of the battlements should be made possible, with the provision of appropriate safety devices, such as railings and stairs.

5 *Lighting.* The walls should be floodlit (with the light fixtures hidden). Street lighting should be subtle, so as not to distract from the illuminated wall. The standard mercury lights should be kept away from the walls. Neon advertisement should be rigidly banned. Power and telephone lines should be kept underground. High tension towers, poles and masts should be kept outside the area.

Road Network

1 *Traffic.* The construction of major arteries within the park would cover a large part of the most beautiful areas and hopelessly ruin the landscape. It is therefore strongly urged that all arteries be located outside the park area. Roads in the park should serve only the park and the Old City and be suitably designed. Large intersections of the clover-leaf' type or even major level crossings should be avoided or relegated to areas outside the park.

2 *Public Transportation.* In the future, the regular road system is likely to prove inadequate. It is not too early to consider some other means of public transportation. The effect of these means on the landscape should be the most important criterion for the choice of the system.

3 *Parkways.* Roads in the park should be of the 'parkway' type. They should be designed as pleasure drives so as to provide the best views. The layout should be such as not to disrupt the landscape. To this end, viaducts, tunnels and split-level roads should be considered. Special concern should be given to the 'finish' of the structures, i.e., stone walls, side slopes, treatment of shoulders and ditches. Roadside parking-bays for viewing the scenery from the car should be provided, wherever possible. The main criterion for the layout of the road network should be the preservation of the landscape — even at the cost of narrower and steeper roads.

4 *Parking.* The area within the park that is available for public use is very limited. With the rapid growth of traffic it is impossible to satisfy all parking needs by using only surface parking. In order to avoid the progressive encroachment of parking areas on land available for rest and recreation, a rigid limit should be imposed on the area allotted to parking. If additional parking space is needed, it should be located outside the park area or be met by underground or multi-storey parking structures.

Five major parking areas should be provided at or near the main gates: west of Damascus Gate, west of Jaffa Gate, near Mount Zion Gate, near the Dung Gate, east of the Lions' Gate.

Minor parking places should be planned near such points of interest as Absalom's Tomb, the Virgin's Fountain, the Pool of Siloam, Acoldama, Observation Point at the Intercontinental Hotel, St Peter in Gallicantu, Arts and Crafts Centre (Huzot Hayotzer), Mishkanot Sha'ananim, Abu Tor and the windmill.

Conventional street parking should be prohibited. The first aim of planned parking is to keep the roads clear to provide an unobstructed view of the landscape.

5 *Parking Lot Design.* The principal aim of planned parking should be to de-emphasise and conceal parking lots, as far as possible. This may be done by breaking the areas into small units, by using terraces to break the level and by planting trees both to conceal the vehicles and provide continuity of the landscape. Large, flat stretches of uninterrupted asphalt lots would be an eyesore. Underground parking should also be considered.

Pedestrians

1 *Pedestrian Routes.* Many visitors walk in and around the Old City for pleasure, study and religious pilgrimage. To all, traffic, particularly on the Sabbath, is distasteful. Pedestrian routes should therefore be kept separate from vehicular traffic. Where traffic roads and pedestrian routes cross, a two-level crossing (bridge or underpass) should be provided. Where the routes are parallel, efforts could be made to keep them on split levels, separated by planted islands.

2 *Promenade.* The entire area between the city walls and the street running from the Rockefeller Museum through Damascus Gate and Jaffa Gate around to Mount Zion should be conceived as one continuous promenade. This promenade should be thought of in imaginative terms with diverse functions, serving the casual stroller, crowded gatherings on festive days and even as the site of open-air art shows. Simple treatment is an essential condition. The promenade should be sufficiently wide, with broad paved areas.

3 *Entrance Piazzas.* Entrance piazzas should be laid out in front of the Jaffa, Damascus, Lions', Herod and Dung Gates. These should be kept free of parked cars and taxis, for their object is to provide a proper setting for, and offer an unrestricted view of, the gates.

4 *The System of Paths.* The paths should afford access to all points of interest, and do so without requiring the visitor to backtrack. They should therefore be designed on the closed-loop principle, rather than as a series of dead-end tracks, each branch serving an individal site. Loop paths would also bind the various sites and provide a harmonious, pleasing and logical route.

5 *Routes Related to Specific Themes.* In designing the system of paths, it might be useful to arrange that each set of paths serve a group of historic sites which share a common theme. For example, a tour of the city's ancient water sources would require paths linking the Gihon Spring (Virgin's Fountain), its underground channel, access shafts, the 600-yard rock-hewn conduit of Hezekiah (eighth–seventh century BC), the pool of Siloam and the Old Pool, with water sources and aqueducts of the Second Temple, Roman and Ottoman periods, from Solomon's Pools, Sultan's Pool and Mamilla Pool to the ancient underground water-holes discovered beneath the Haram esh-Sharif.

6 *Observation Platforms.* Scenic observation points should be established at sites which offer the best views. These should be designed to accommodate groups of visitors at a time (at least a bus load) and should provide some sort of shade, benches, drinking fountains and visual aids (maps, pointers, etc.). Public conveniences and soft-drink kiosks should be planned at the more popular observation points.

1 *Paving along the northern city wall*
2–4 *Terraced walk on the southern slopes of Kidron Valley. Great care was taken to preserve the character of original terrain*

Building and Zoning

1 *Building Limitations.* As a general principle, construction of new buildings in the park should be prohibited. Exceptions should be made for the three following categories:

a. Buildings which provide immediate services for visitors, such as coffee shops, souvenir stores, public conveniences, etc. However, service buildings which by their very character or size (gasoline stations, etc.) would spoil the landscape should be excluded.

b. Cultural buildings, such as museums, galleries, artists' studios, craftsmen's workshops, may be permitted in appropriate sites.

c. Religious buildings, provided they are in scale with the surrounding landscape.

2 *Architectural Ensembles* should be preserved by appropriate ordinances. There exist three such ensembles in the area:

a. Yemin Moshe and Mishkenot Sha'ananim, the first Jewish settlement outside the walls, built by Sir Moses Montefiore. Planning for the restoration of the area has already begun, and the reconstruction of some of the houses is almost completed.

b. Some parts of Shama'a in the Valley of Hinnom.

c. The village of Siloam. Although it is not proposed to include the village within the park boundaries, special attention should be given to its preservation.

3 *Building in Stone.* One of the safest means to achieve a harmony between the styles of the various areas is to insist that all buildings be of stone. (Those parts of Jerusalem where building with stone is compulsory offer vivid testimony to to the validity of the principle.) We recognise that this ordinance limits somewhat the architectural possibilities; but the boon to landscape protection vastly outweighs this cost.

4 *The Ophel Area.* This is the site of the City of David, and it is of great archaeological importance. A nondescript neighbourhood has recently sprung up here, with many ugly buildings, lacking the picturesque charm of the neighbouring village of Siloam. Since the resettlement of hundreds of families is an extremely expensive task, the liquidation of this neighbourhood should be thought of in terms of a long-range policy: no new building should be permitted, plots should be gradually purchased and families relocated in new areas.

5 *The Skyline.* New building on the ridges around the Old City should be examined for its effect on the skyline. Small to meduim buildings, mosques and church towers present little danger but monumental buildings may ruin the harmony. Most of the surrounding hill tops are crowned by dark clusters of pine and cypress trees which are of major importance in shaping the skyline, as exemplified by the groves of Augusta Victoria, Viri Gallilaei, Government House Hill and Mount Zion. Other locations on the ring of surrounding hills may benefit from similar emphasis.

Planting

1 *The Valley Belt.* The valley belt is the dominant ring which skirts the Old City around the west and south (Valley of Hinnom) and the east (Kidron Valley). Within this belt of valleys are olive groves, orchards of fig, vine and date palms and vegetable patches between trees. The proposed park and garden areas will intermingle with the existing plantations.

2 *The Forest Belt.* The forest belt runs along the slopes on both sides of the valleys forming the valley belt, though it is very intermittent, with large gaps of treeless areas. Where there are trees, they are unlike those in the valleys, most of them following the vertical form — pines and cypresses. Dark green is the prevailing colour. The slopes of Mount Zion are in need of afforestation, which should match the pattern and colour of the existing parts of the forest belt.

3 *The Belt Skirting the Walls.* The third belt is the strip adjoining the walls, covered with native grass, wild flowers and shrubs — all of them low plants which should be kept low, so as not to hide the full view of the walls. Special thought should be given to the ecological balance. With the disappearance of grazing animals from the area, whose cropping kept the natural vegetation low and neat, tall weeds have sprung up, which are ugly and unsightly and which present a fire hazard.

4 *Avenues of Trees.* Rows of trees, notably cypresses, lining avenues and fences are a characteristic landscape feature of Jerusalem. They create a harmonious sense of rhythm, direction and line. They also provide pleasant shade. Much use should be made of this element. Apart from cypress trees, pine, carob and olive trees would admirably suit this purpose.

5 *The Colour Scheme.* The colour scheme should be limited to green, with variations of shade — from silvery olive to very dark cypress. However, occasional patches of brilliant colour, boldly used, could well fit the landscape and reflect the Mediterranean character of the region. A positive example of this is the brilliant purple bougainvillaea near Gethsemane. The colour scheme of the local wild flowers could be studied and reinforced or changed if necessary.

6 *Light and Shade.* The special interplay of light and shade is characteristic of the region. It is most important that the planting of trees should follow a loose arrangement, with thickets and open spaces so juxtaposed that the tall trees throw long shadows on the open areas. Immediately to the east of Jerusalem lies the Judean Desert, and care should be taken in the afforestation plan not to conflict too greatly with the general landscape.

The park is located within the municipal boundaries of the City of Jerusalem. But it is more than a municipal park. It must serve the entire nation, as well as tourists and pilgrims from many lands. The enormous burden of establishing and maintaining the park should therefore be borne by the whole nation, and government and other national (and possibly international) funds should be made available. The responsibility for the design and establishment of the park should be shared by a joint team of the National Parks Authority and the City of Jerusalem.

opposite *Ancient graves carved in the cliffs*

1 Siloam village
2 St Mary Magdalene, the Russian
Church on the slopes of the Mount
of Olives
3 Sultan's sybil (drinking place)

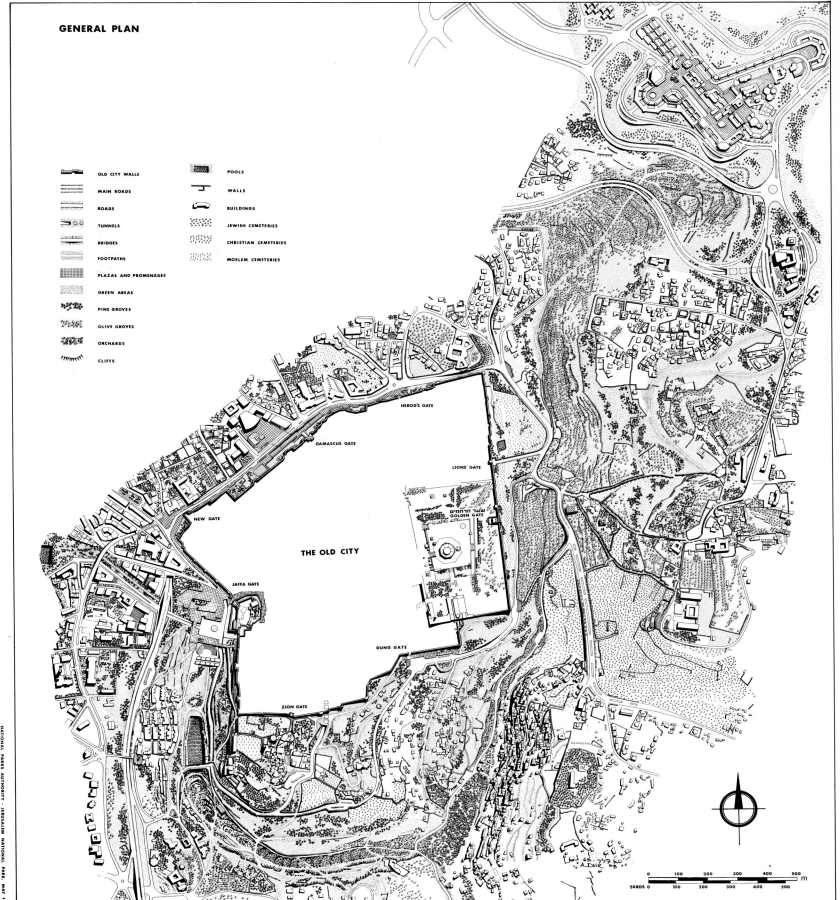

GENERAL PLAN

OLD CITY WALLS

MAIN ROADS

ROADS

TUNNELS

BRIDGES

FOOTPATHS

PLAZAS AND PROMENADES

GREEN AREAS

PINE GROVES

OLIVE GROVES

ORCHARDS

CLIFFS

POOLS

WALLS

BUILDINGS

JEWISH CEMETERIES

CHRISTIAN CEMETERIES

MOSLEM CEMETERIES

THE OLD CITY

HEROD'S GATE

DAMASCUS GATE

LIONS' GATE

NEW GATE

GOLDEN GATE

JAFFA GATE

DUNG GATE

ZION GATE

NATIONAL PARKS AUTHORITY · JERUSALEM NATIONAL PARK, MAY 1969.

YARDS 0   100   200   300   400   500

0   100   200   300   400   500 m

207

Acknowledgements

The Outline Townplanning Scheme for the Old City of Jerusalem and its Environs was commissioned by the Ministry of the Interior and the Municipality of Jerusalem and devised (during the years 1968–70) by the architects and townplanners Arieh Sharon, David Anatol Brutzkus and Eldar Sharon.

They take this opportunity of acknowledging the important contribution made by the principal specialist members of the team they headed: economist Doron Klinghofer, who was in charge of the surveys and administration; architects Shlomo Khayat, Ezra Sharon and Benjamin Muchawsky; geographers Tsipora Klein-Sigan and Abraham Landau; designer Chava Mordohovich; draughts-women Tsipora Segal, Tamar Pfeniger and Miryam Nir; and the secretary, Haya Fleury-Masheioff.

In the preparation of this book, I have received help from government ministries, the Jerusalem Municipality and public institutions. To all I owe a debt of gratitude. Of particular value was the data supplied by the Planning Department of the Ministry of the Interior and by the Departments of the City Engineer.

I wish to thank Mr Ya'akov Dash and Mr Ammikam Yafeh, who were kind enough to read the manuscript and offer helpful advice. Special thanks go to architect Shlomo Khayat, who was also responsible for the detailed survey of the Old City and devoted much of his time to this publication;to Mily Eytan, who worked on the drawings and preparation of the maps; to architect Peter Bugod, who prepared the survey on the Gates of the Old City; to Dan Bahad, who was responsible for the historical maps; to Johanan Mintzker, who helped in the location and listing of historical, religious and architectural sites in the Old City; and to Yael Aloni, whose general editorial help was invaluable.

The photographs which illustrate this book were taken by: Nir Bareket, Werner Braun, Hanna and Efraim Degani, Photo Garo, David Hadar, David Harris, Judy and Kenny Lester, Chava Mordohovich and Pantomap. My thanks to them all.

I also thank the Israel Museum, the National Library and the National Parks Authority for permission to reproduce maps and illustrations from their collections.

Jerusalem
February 1973   Arieh Sharon

Selected Bibliography

Architecture in Israel, *Journal of the Association of Engineers and Architects in Israel, No. 6, October-December 1968.*

Avi-Yonah, Michael, ed., A History of the Holy Land, *Jerusalem (Steimatzky's Agency and Weidenfeld and Nicolson),* 1968.

Avi-Yonah, Michael, ed., Sepher Yerushalayim — *The Book of Jerusalem (Hebrew), Jerusalem-Tel Aviv (The Bialik Institute and Dvir Publishing House), 1956.*

Bahad, Dan, ed., Yerushalayim Letkufoteia — Jerusalem Throughout the Ages *(Hebrew), Jerusalem (Carta), 1969.*

Brutzkus, Eliezer, Jerusalem Masterplan — A Critical Appraisal, *1970.*

Cohen, M., The Tombs of the Kings *(Hebrew), Tel Aviv (Dvir Publishing House), 1946.*

Dash, Jacob B. and Elisha Efrat, The Israel Physical Master Plan, *Jerusalem (Ministry of the Interior Planning Department), 1964.*

Dvir, Arye, Jerusalem National Park, *Preliminary Proposal by the National Parks Authority.*

Hashimshony, A., Joseph Schweid and Zion Hashimshony, Interim Report — The Masterplan 1968, *Jerusalem (Municipality of Jerusalem),* 1970.

Kendall, Harry, Jerusalem, The City Plan — Preservation and Development During the British Mandate, 1918–1948, *London (His Majesty's Stationery Office), 1948.*

Kenyon, Kathleen, Jerusalem — Excavating 3000 Years of History, *London (Thames and Hudson), 1967.*

Kollek, Teddy and Moshe Pearlman, Jerusalem, *Jerusalem (Steimatzky's Agency and Weidenfeld and Nicolson), 1968.*

National Parks Authority, The Gates of Jerusalem, *April 1969.*

Old City of Jerusalem and Its Environs Design Team, Old City of Jerusalem — Bazaars and Commercial Streets.

Pearlman, Moshe and Yaacov Yannai, Historical Sites in Israel, *Tel Aviv-Jerusalem (Massada — P.E.C. Press Ltd.), 1964.*

Sharon, Arieh, Physical Planning in Israel, *Jerusalem (The Government Printer), 1951.*

Sharon Arieh, David Anatol Brutzkus and Eldar Sharon, Old City of Jerusalem and its Environs — Outline Townplanning Scheme 1970, *Jerusalem (Jerusalem Committee), November 1970.*

Smith, George Adam, Jerusalem: From the Earliest Times to AD 70, *London (Hodder and Stoughton), 1907.*